originalstrength
PERFORMANCE
THE NEXT LEVEL

By Tim Anderson,
Chip Morton, and
Mark Shropshire

Original Strength Performance: The Next Level
by Tim Anderson, Chip Morton, and Mark Shropshire

Copyright © 2018 Original Strength Systems, LLC

All rights reserved solely by the copyright holder. The copyright holder guarantees all contents are original and do not infringe upon the legal rights of any other person or work. No part of this book may be reproduced or transmitted in any form or by any means, electronic or mechanical, including photocopying, recording or by any information storage and retrieval system, without the permission of the copyright holder.

Published by OS Press

Edition ISBNs:
Hardcover: 978-1-64184-931-9
Paperback: 978-1-64184-932-6
ebook: 978-1-64184-933-3

First Edition 2018
Printed in the United States of America

Unless otherwise indicated, Bible quotations are taken from the New King James Version. Copyright © 1982 by Thomas Nelson, Inc. Used by permission. All rights reserved.

Thank you to JETLAUNCH.net for editing and book design.

TABLE OF CONTENTS

CHAPTER 1: WHAT IS PERFORMANCE? 1

   Improving Human Performance. 2

   Original Strength and Performance 3

CHAPTER 2: THE THREE PILLARS OF HUMAN MOVEMENT. 7

   Pillar #1: Breathing with the Diaphragm 8

   Pillar #2: Activating the Vestibular System Appropriately 10

   Pillar #3: Contra-lateral Patterns and the X 12

CHAPTER 3: THE ROOTS OF PERFORMANCE. 15

   The Taproot. 19

   Loading the Gait Pattern 22

      Using a Harness. 23

      Using Rucksacks and Weight Vests 25

      Loading the Limbs. 27

Chapter 4: The Trunk of Strength 31

Loading the X 32
- The Cross-body Single Leg Deadlift (SLDL) 33
- The Getup 34
- True Strength Vs Pretty Muscles 37

Building Old Man Strength for Optimal Performance 38
- Heavy Carry Day! 42
- Manpower and Sleds 46

We Were Made to Move 48
- Move More, Move Better 49
- The Major Human Movement Patterns 50

Chapter 5: The Branches of Expression 65

Recovering to Perform 66

Original Strength and the Nervous System: Optimizing Performance and Health 68
- The Central Nervous System 70
- The Peripheral Nervous System 74

The Human Body's Stress Response 83
- Adrenaline 84
- Cortisol 84
- Mitigating the Human Stress Response 87
- Regularly Participate in a Stress-Relieving Activity (Press RESET) 90
- The Human Stress Response Can Also Be Good ...91

THE GREATEST PERFORMANCE VARIABLE 99

    The Three Keys to LEAD 100

    LEAD 103

IN THE END 105

BIBLIOGRAPHY 107

ABOUT THE AUTHORS 109

DISCLAIMER!

You must get your physician's approval before beginning this exercise program.

These recommendations are not medical guidelines but are for educational purposes only. You must consult your physician prior to starting this program or if you have any medical condition or injury that is contraindicated to performing physical activity. This program is designed for healthy individuals 18 years and older only.

See your physician before starting any exercise or nutrition program. If you are taking any medications, you must talk to your physician before starting any exercise program, including the Original Strength program. If you experience any lightheadedness, dizziness, or shortness of breath while exercising, stop the movement and consult a physician.

It is strongly recommended that you have a complete physical examination if you live a sedentary lifestyle, have high cholesterol, high blood pressure, diabetes, are overweight, or if you are over 30 years old. Please discuss all nutritional changes with your physician or a registered dietitian. If your physician recommends that you not use the Original Strength program, please follow your doctor's orders.

All forms of exercise pose some inherent risks. The authors, editors and publishers advise readers to take full responsibility for their own safety and know their limits. When using the exercises in this program, do not take risks beyond your level of experience, aptitude, training and fitness. The exercises and dietary programs in this program are not intended as a substitute for any exercise routine, treatment or dietary regimen prescribed by your physician.

Having said all of that, this is not an exercise book. The movements in this book are the movements you have already made, and they are the movements that you probably should be making every day. For example, we introduce breathing in this book. If your doctor advises against breathing, you should probably seek out another doctor, or at least ask for a second opinion!

There is a small exercise section in this book, but the book itself is intended to help you remember how you were designed to move. Again, this is not an exercise book. This is a movement restoration book. Enjoy!

1

WHAT IS PERFORMANCE?

"What you look at will determine what you see. What you see through will determine how you see."

—Wayne Dyer

This book is about improving your performance as an athlete, a coach, a trainer, and a person. This is not solely a book about improving athletic performance, although that is a huge focus. Rather, this book is about improving life performance.

But I'm getting ahead of myself. First, what exactly is *performance*? The dictionary defines performance as the action or process of carrying out or accomplishing an action, task, or function. So, performance is task, action, or function-specific, and it is measured by the completion, execution, or effectiveness of the action being carried out. In other words, performance is a presentation of execution, and it is often a rated presentation. We rate performance by how well something was done. We say things like, "He performed poorly," or "He's a real performer," or "That quarterback sucks," etc. . . .

As stated above, this book is about helping you improve your performance in life; on and off the field, in the office and in the home, in the company of friends or colleagues and when you're alone. If performance is a rated presentation of execution, then our goal is to help you live your life well. Now, don't roll your eyes just yet. There is going to be a lot of talk about strength training in this book. The training methods and techniques in this book will make you as strong as you want to be, but strength is only one variable of performance. And if we are going to aim at improving your athletic performance—and really, your life performance—then we also have to acknowledge those other variables as well.

Strength is not performance; strength is a variable that affects performance. But remember, performance is action or task-specific. This is an important knowledge nugget because in the world of strength training, much lip service is given to improving athletic performance. But, that is often just what it is: lip service. Too often, what is meant by improving athletic performance is only a quest to enhance weight-room performance. And make no mistake about it, weight-room performance does not equate to athletic performance. Many people train themselves to perform well in the weight room, but they have a hard time even walking up a set of stairs. Their prowess in the weight room does little to improve their quality of life or their performance on the field.

Let's look at the other variables of performance.

Improving Human Performance

It may help to look at performance as a symphony. Many instruments make up the symphony, but there are also many hours of practice, dedication, effort, and talent necessary. There is also song selection and theme. All of these variables come together to create the musical masterpiece that is played and enjoyed. Athletic performance is no different, and it has its own variables.

How one performs athletically, or in life, is ultimately an expression of their reflexive control, their mental and emotional state, their level of physical fitness and preparedness, their level of mental tenacity and focus, their talent, and their belief. This is not even close to an exhaustive list, but I think you get the point. Human performance is an expression of what's inside. What's inside the athlete relates to what's inside their body, their mind, their genes, and their heart. It involves what comes from them intrinsically and what comes into them externally. What they believe, what they hear, what they see, how they move, how they train, how they sleep—these all matter, and they are all woven together to create the performance that will be expressed.

Improve any of these variables, and you improve them all, along with the overall performance of the individual. Conversely, damage any of these variables, and you also take away from the overall performance of the person. The human body is an interwoven tapestry, a masterpiece of variables.

With so many variables, some that can be targeted and others that can't, where do you start if you are trying to improve human performance? It's simple; you start with the variable that has the greatest effect on all of the other variables: movement.

Original Strength and Performance

You should know by now that the body was designed to move in specific ways intended to give it an Original Strength, a foundation of reflexive control. If you don't know this, please reference the book, *Pressing RESET: Original Strength Reloaded*. Reflexive control is the body's ability to express itself in mobility, strength, speed, fluidity, and grace. The better a person's reflexive control, the better their mental and emotional state. The more reflexive control a person has, the better their performance potential.

When a person lacks reflexive control, they will have movement barriers and limitations. These limitations will result in movement compensations and even mental frustrations. Movement compensations are the brain's way of trying to achieve a result, a physical expression, through limited means. These limited means may get the job done, but the job may not be done well, or the way it is done can increase the risk of injury.

When a person has a great amount of reflexive control, they are free to move and express themselves physically. They have optimal stability, mobility, posture, coordination, and strength. In other words, they move well with efficiency, and their body is more resilient because it doesn't need to call upon compensations to get things done.

Another advantage to having a depth of reflexive control is that it allows the body to have an effortless "movement vocabulary," allowing for quick learning and skill acquisition. The ability to move well lends itself to being able to think and concentrate well. It enables an athlete to see a movement or a drill and learn it almost instantly. This can happen because there are no movement limitations that have to be overcome, nor are there mental frustrations that tend to accompany these movement barriers. An athlete that is free to express themselves is an athlete that is free to absorb and learn.

To be crystal clear, athletic performance is not isolated to the field of play, unless of course, the "field of play" is life in the world. Every human ever born was a born athlete. We all are. To improve athletic performance is to improve life, and the benefits are far greater than any highlights of a sports career. Being able to walk down your own driveway at age 88 with the same ease you did at age 49 is athletic performance. Being able to put on your own pants while standing or being able to tie your own shoes while standing is athletic performance. These things that make life easier are all athletically performance based. Having reflexive strength is what gives us the ability to live life like a performance. Regaining reflexive strength, if we've lost it, is what allows us to perform an encore. Great athletes always get back up. Right?

So, where does this depth of reflexive strength come from? And can it be developed?

Yes, it can. And it can be as simple as following The Three Pillars of Original Strength. Really, these are The Three Pillars of Human Movement. They are essential to optimal human expression and performance:

1) Breathe properly using the diaphragm

2) Activate the vestibular system appropriately.

3) Engage in contra-lateral and midline crossing movements

Let's take a more in-depth look at these pillars.

2

THE THREE PILLARS OF HUMAN MOVEMENT

". . . Though the rain comes in torrents and the floodwaters rise and the winds beat against that house, it won't collapse because it is built on bedrock."

—Matthew 7:25

To optimally perform in life and on the field, the body needs to have a very efficient and healthy nervous system, a nervous system that is quick to both react and predict the movements it needs to make. This means all of the "switches" in the nervous system need to be "on." Everything in the body has to do its job and uphold its end of the bargain by giving the brain accurate information about what the body is doing and needs to be doing so the brain can return appropriate commands to the body so it can perform. Again, optimal performance is about efficiency and accuracy of information traveling to the brain from the body and from the brain to the body. It's about having a healthy nervous system, which is the same thing as having Original Strength, or reflexive control. They are the same.

The way to turn on all of the "switches" in the nervous system and keep the nervous system healthy is through living inside the three pillars of human movement. We were designed to do this continually throughout life.

Pillar #1: Breathing with the Diaphragm

Breathing with the diaphragm is where we begin creating an efficient nervous system. Breathing is not only about the gas exchange between oxygen and carbon dioxide. That is important, but it's just a part of the whole symphony. Breathing is about the health of the entire tapestry known as man. The mind, the emotions, the nervous system, the autonomic nervous system, the immune system, the digestive system—*name a system*—they are all affected by how you breathe.

Everything about you is affected by how you breathe, especially your strength and performance potential. In fact, strength and performance start here. The diaphragm, your breathing muscle, is a spinal stabilizer. It gives stability (protection) to the spine. It may also help to imagine it to be the Captain of the Spinal Stabilizers, an awesome movie title coming soon to a theatre near you. The diaphragm is neurologically connected to the other spinal stabilizers: the pelvic floor, the transverse abdominus, the multifidi, the psoas, and the quadratus lumborum. These muscles all have a job to do, to stabilize the spine. They are designed to work together. But, as the captain, the diaphragm is in charge. If the diaphragm is appropriately used, filling the lungs up from the bottom to the top, it is creating spinal stability and inner core strength through a coordinated effort from the other spinal stabilizers. However, if the diaphragm is dysfunctional, not being used correctly, it can also lead to other issues of dysfunction like a pelvic floor disorder. Think of it this way: dysfunction = weakness (or worse, pain).

Why is spinal stability so important? Well, it keeps you safe. A stable spine leads to a mobile and agile body. When the brain knows the spine is protected, the brain is free to tell other muscles how to do their primary jobs. On the other hand, if the brain doesn't trust that the spinal stabilizers are doing their jobs, it may recruit other muscles to stabilize the spine, primary movement muscles not designed for stabilizing. The result is movement compensation and limitation.

In another example, walk down the "what if" road with me. What if the root of one person's back pain was because they were continually breathing with their accessory breathing muscles and never employing the diaphragm to do its job? What if their dysfunctional diaphragm also leads to their spinal stabilizers' inability to perform their job well, so the brain decides to use bigger muscles, like the glutes, to stabilize the spine? What kind of movement compensations or pain will result when the brain tries to use the powerful glutes to stabilize the spine? Just something to ponder on.

Breathing correctly with the diaphragm is not just about stabilizing the spine, either. As stated above, everything about you is affected by how you breathe. As it turns out, how you breathe dramatically affects your autonomic nervous system (your sympathetic and parasympathetic nervous systems—your "fight or flight" nervous system and your "rest and digest" nervous system). The diaphragm is also neurologically connected to the vagal nerve and how you breathe can determine your vagal tone. The vagal nerve is the nerve that can toggle you back and forth between "fight or flight" mode and "rest and digest" mode. Vagal tone is how your heart rate responds when you breathe in versus when you breathe out. The higher your vagal tone, the faster your body can recover. This is important because if an athlete cannot recover, his performance will suffer. Being able to enter the parasympathetic mode—being able to rest, digest, and recover—is pivotal for optimal human expression and performance. How a person breathes dramatically determines how a person recovers.

The interworkings and weavings of the diaphragm are way more miraculous and complicated than I have mentioned here. The truth is, I'm not even scratching the surface yet. My goal right now is to illustrate the importance of breathing properly for strength and health in a simple, digestible manner. The takeaway is that a properly functioning diaphragm is essential for strength and health as it lays the foundation for optimal human performance and physical expression. Trying to perform well without breathing correctly is like trying to play football on shifting sand while wearing snorkel gear. You can do it, but it's not the best.

Pillar #2: Activating the Vestibular System Appropriately

The vestibular system (VS) resides in the head behind the ears. In Original Strength, we teach that the VS is the star of the show because all of the information the body receives and makes (minus smell) gets routed through the vestibular system before it enters the brain. The better the information that is received and detected by the VS, the better the response commands that are sent out from the brain. Optimal information into the VS and then into the brain, leads to optimal action and reaction from the brain.

At least, that is how it should work. But the VS itself needs stimulation to remain healthy. In other words, it needs to be exercised and stimulated on a regular basis. The VS is our internal gyroscopic system. One of its primary jobs is to level our heads with the horizon. It is designed to detect head motion in all plains of motion: linear, rotation, and angular.

Another main role of the VS, related to keeping the head on the horizon, is to protect the head. After all, this is where the brain lives. For the VS to remain healthy, it needs to be used; it needs to detect head motion. In other words, we are designed to move our heads, and we should move them to stay healthy, as well as provide ourselves with the best opportunity to thrive and survive through life's situations. The key to exercising and fine-tuning our vestibular system is first through head movement, followed by body movement. This keeps the VS "sharp," which in turn keeps the entire body sharp because the nervous system is getting and giving good information.

The goal is to give good information, appropriate information, through our preprogrammed movement template. What do I mean by appropriate information? Well, it is easy to activate the VS. All you have to do is move or be moved. Sitting on a washing machine will activate the VS, but it may not optimize your performance. Standing on a BOSU® ball while performing single leg squats is cool, but it may not be the best way to supply the VS with information. In other words, there are ways to send a flood of chaotic information through the VS, but remember that one of the primary jobs of the VS is to protect your head and keep your head level with the horizon, on a stable world, with a constant force of gravity. If the information is chaotic and doesn't relate to the world you were designed to live in, it may not be the best or most appropriate information to be sending your brain to achieve optimal human performance in a world that humans were built for. Make sense?

This is of utmost importance for anyone who wants to live their life well, or anyone who wants to improve their performance. To perform at our best, it is essential to have a healthy VS and to also supply it with appropriate information and as much complete information as possible.

Appropriate *and* complete? Okay, pay attention. The VS gives the brain the information it receives. Therefore, if the brain is to get the best picture so that it can give the best response to the body, the VS and the brain need to receive the whole picture, not just parts of the picture. One way to ensure that your VS is getting all of the information you can give it is to keep your tongue where it belongs, on the roof of your mouth behind your front teeth. This simple act, or home position of the tongue, gives complete information to the VS, and it allows your neck to move your head with less effort. It also helps the diaphragm perform its job properly as well. Remember Pillar #1?

This tiny muscle makes the input received by the nervous system more complete, and the results are astounding. In fact, a recent study demonstrated that placing the tongue on the roof of the mouth improved force production and endurance in flexion and extension.[1] Yes, it may seem crazy, but the simple act of keeping your tongue on the roof of your mouth is a true performance enhancer. If you only engaged in this, out of everything else presented in this book, it would change your life forever. Don't miss this!

This is probably also the best place to mention that the other two Pillars of Human Movement work best when all three pillars are combined or engaged in at the same time. Any one of them on their own is good, but all three together is best. I mention this here because keeping your tongue on the roof of your mouth while breathing with the diaphragm, and engaging in contra-lateral patterns, while you are activating your VS, is the best way to provide your VS and brain with the complete information. It's the best way to ensure a healthy, efficient nervous system and build a foundation of reflexive control.

We will discuss this in more depth, but first, let's talk about Pillar #3.

Pillar #3: Contra-lateral Patterns and the X

The human body was designed to move from one place to another through a contra-lateral movement pattern. That is, when you walk, your opposite limbs should move together in coordination with one another. This contra-lateral movement pattern is the movement that was designed to keep you able and ready to perform in life at any age. This is the pattern that ties your X together. Let me explain.

The body is an X. In fact, it's a series of Xs in both shape and working design. It is designed to move contra-laterally, with opposing limbs working together in coordinated rhythmic fashion. Think of the top right side of the X being connected to the left bottom side of the X, just as you would imagine an X to be connected. In the middle is the torso, where the lines cross. This is where all of the real action takes place physically, even though that is the part that doesn't seem to be moving as much as the limbs. The center of the X is where the forces we generate and encounter get transmitted to the other side. The stronger the center, the better the X moves, and the more resilient the X is because the forces it generates travel through it efficiently.

The theme of the X is also deeper than the physical appearance of the body. For some reason, the right hemisphere of the brain controls the left side of the body, and the left hemisphere of the brain controls the right side of the body. Neurologically, deeper than the appearance, the body is still an X. When we crawl, march, or walk and run as we should, both hemispheres of the brain communicate and work together to coordinate the opposing limb patterns. Our gait pattern makes the brain and nervous system very efficient because that pattern continually makes the whole brain communicate with itself and with the body. This establishes very fast and efficient neural pathways. The more efficient these pathways are, the healthier the brain becomes and the better the X moves.

Physically speaking, the X, the human body, moves best when it is physically and neurologically tied together in the center. Strong centers and efficient nervous systems are built and established from engaging in our contra-lateral patterns, adding loads to the opposing contra-lateral limbs, and crossing midline from one side of the body to the other. Think touching your right arm to your left knee.

Again, the best way to optimize human athletic performance and potential is to engage in all Three Pillars of Human Movement at the same time. An example of this would be crawling with the head held up on the horizon, the tongue on the roof of the mouth while breathing diaphragmatically through the nose. Living *in* the Three Pillars is the foundation of reflexive control; it develops the roots of all human expression.

3

THE ROOTS OF PERFORMANCE

"And he looked up and said, 'I see men like trees, walking.'"

—Mark 8:24

In my mind, it helps to think of a tree when trying to understand human expression (human performance). I like to think of the roots of the tree as the nervous system of the body. The deeper the roots run and the thicker they are, the bigger the tree they can support. I see the trunk of the tree as the body, the structure. The trunk (the body) can become big and strong on top of a deep, efficient, nourishing root system (nervous system). Then I see the branches and all they yield—the leaves, the flowers, the fruit, the place for critters, etc.—as the expressions the body is capable of making. Performance is expression. The deeper the roots, the bigger the structure, the greater the expressions can be. In other words, the healthier the nervous system is, the more resilient the body can be, and the better the body can perform in every area.

In looking at the picture of the tree below, notice how the branches (the expressions) mirror the roots (the nervous system). How one performs or expresses themselves is ultimately a reflection of the state of their nervous system. Building a healthy nervous system starts and ends with engaging in the Three Pillars of Human Movement, by Pressing RESET. Breathing, controlling the movements of the head, rolling, rocking, and the gait pattern—these are RESETs. They honor the Pillars. They develop and nourish the "roots" of performance.

We can develop and nourish the roots by engaging in the Three Pillars and Pressing RESET, but can we strengthen them and make them thicker, capable of supporting a more resilient body to improve or unlock performance? Can we deepen the foundation of reflexive control? Yes, we can.

The truth is that simply engaging in all Three Pillars of Human Movement at the same time will develop and keep the nervous system healthy. This alone will improve the performance of anyone as it helps them to live their life better. But, if we add load or resistance to all Three Pillars, then we have now placed a demand on the nervous system that will have to be adapted to, especially if we are consistent with the load we are adding. Indeed, adding load to the Three Pillars is also double dipping; it also strengthens the structure. But, what it does to the root system, the nervous system, is provide a lot more information to the brain that requires a bigger response from the brain. Adding resistance (not necessarily weight) elicits a greater neuro-muscular response that, over time and through consistent engagement, will make the nervous system even more efficient at generating the higher output. What I'm trying to say is that adding an appropriate load to the Pillars of Human Movement gives you even faster, more efficient, neural pathways while adding strength to the entire structure.

The key is adding an appropriate load. Too much of a good thing can become, well, you know . . . A little bit of vitamin C can keep a cold away. A lotta bit of vitamin C can keep you away, in the bathroom, with diarrhea . . .

How do you know what the appropriate load is?

The answer will be individual specific, but in general, an appropriate load often enhances or improves the movement being loaded. Again, don't think weight training here. Think of natural human movement. The positive effect of an appropriate load can easily be seen when looking at the Three Pillars of Human Movement. For example, a person may be crawling but have the inability to keep their head up, their back flat, or even engage in a contra-lateral pattern. A light load of weight or resistance placed on their head could immediately cause their head to rise and become level with the horizon, their back to become flat and strong, and their contra-lateral pattern to become present and fluid. All of these improvements in movement come because an appropriate load stimulates a higher neurological output to the body.

If, however, a heavier load was placed on the same person and the crawling pattern breaks down and the posture of the person becomes worse, the load is too great; it's not appropriate for that person. When you add load to a natural human movement and the movement improves, consider that load or resistance to be an appropriate load. When you add load to natural human movement, and the movement degrades, consider that load to be an inappropriate load.

To offer one more example where appropriate versus inappropriate load is easily visible, consider the farmer's carry. If a person grabs two somewhat heavy dumbbells and goes for a walk, the weight of the dumbbells often elicits a beneficial response in the person's posture; they stand perfectly tall, and all their bones and joints stack up on top of each other. They look great! But, if that same person grabs two extremely heavy dumbbells and goes for a walk, the weight of the dumbbells—if it is too heavy for that individual—degrades their posture, causing their spine to round, their head to jut out, and their gait pattern to become short, uneven, un-rhythmic, and choppy.

The right load can enhance movement while it strengthens the nervous system. The wrong load can degrade movement and also cause the nervous system to learn compensatory movement patterns. There are a few sayings that come to mind: "Nerves that fire together wire together," and "If you want a pattern to stick, add a load to it." In other words, load the body to get the response you want, not the response you don't want, because the body will give you exactly what you ask from it. Do not ask amiss.

THE TAPROOT

The best place to start, when looking to strengthen the roots of performance, is ensuring proper diaphragmatic breathing and then learning how to breathe intentionally under load. The diaphragm is, after all, a muscle; a muscle that can be strengthened along with the nerves that control it.

Adding load to the diaphragm is a hot trend right now in the fitness industry. Elevation training masks are everywhere. The theory behind these masks is very sound; restrict the airflow coming into the lungs, requiring more effort and power to breathe, improving the body's ability to breathe under stress along with enhancing the body's stamina and capacity to get work done. It's a great example of adding a stress to cause an adaptation in the body.

But, how does an elevation mask work on someone who is an accessory muscle breather? Or an open mouth breather? If a person doesn't naturally breathe through their nose with their diaphragm as they should, what does adding a load to their compensatory breathing pattern do for them? Well, more than likely, it reinforces the breathing pattern they already have. Will they be able to last longer in their sport if they become proficient at breathing through the most restricted settings on their elevation mask? Sure. But, would learning, or remembering, how to breathe through the "load" of the smaller nasal passages of the nose by pulling air down into the bottom of the lungs with the diaphragm also allow them to perform better and last longer in their sport? Yes, it absolutely will, perhaps even better than an elevation training mask.

There is scientific evidence to back this up. Nasal breathing increases nitric oxide production in the body.[2] Nitric oxide is not only a vasodilator that helps get more oxygen to the heart and muscles, thus increasing athletic performance potential, but even more fascinating than that, nitric oxide gets more oxygen to the brain by increasing cerebral blood flow.[3] It also acts as a neurotransmitter associated with neural plasticity.[4] This means nasal breathing could not only play a pivotal role in athletic performance enhancement, but it could also play a pivotal role in brain health and brain injury rehabilitation. This means proper breathing, through the nasal passages, may be the first step to keeping the brain healthy and helping the brain heal from a concussion.

So, before the mask, learning how to add natural load to the diaphragm is the first and best place to start when we set out to strengthen our roots. Think of breathing correctly as the "taproot" to your nervous system. Everything else about you will be layered and affected by how you breathe. While breathing through the nose should not be the load we are seeking to add to the diaphragm, it will be for many. And if this is where you, or your athlete, need to start, this is where you should start. Once a person knows how to breathe, we can add a true load to the diaphragm by activating the vestibular system and engaging in contra-lateral movement. We can do this through crawling, marching, or walking.

Crawling lends itself well to strengthening the diaphragm. It allows you to add load and increase the load to breathing through time, distance, direction, and tension. Crawling is also gentle. You can "meet an athlete where they are" with crawling. It is not too strenuous, it won't get the heart rate up too high, and it is easy on the body, yet it can be tough on the mind. This gentle load makes it easier to pull air down into the belly than other activities that might make the heart rate elevate too quickly, either through intensity or perceived threat.

Even though crawling is easy on the body, it will still place a demand on the heart and respiratory rate and a load on the diaphragm, providing the stimulus needed to produce strength and endurance in the diaphragm. Crawling also demands the entire coordinated effort of the body through engaging in the gait pattern, and it helps to set optimal posture (Pillars II and III).

Regardless of whether crawling, marching, walking or any other activity is used to place a demand on the diaphragm to strengthen it, the key to success is keeping the tongue on the roof of the mouth with the jaw and lips relaxed but shut. This technique forces nasal breathing and allows both the coach and the athlete to use the tongue as the governor for diaphragmatic strength training.

For example, if an athlete is trying to cover a certain distance or meet a specific timeframe while crawling, the moment they can no longer keep their mouth shut, the point where they have to gasp for air, is the moment they should rest to allow for recovery until they can close their mouth again. Both time and distance can be logged to keep track of progress with the goal eventually being to be able to perform any activity, even intense ones, with the lips shut and the tongue on the roof of the mouth while nasal breathing deep into the belly.

In case this has crossed your mind, the emergency breathing muscles, the accessory breathing muscles, are to be used in moments of intense action (fight, flight, exhaustion, etc.), but that does not mean the diaphragm should no longer be filling the lungs from the bottom to the top. This can become possible through learning how to breathe properly with the diaphragm in simple activities, which makes it easier to breathe with the diaphragm during difficult and complex activities or moments of intense stress.

Just in case you cannot see or understand how engaging in the gait pattern with the lips shut can be used to strengthen the diaphragm, I encourage you to stop reading this book right now and learn by doing it. Experience what I'm sharing with you by trying one or both of the following:

1) Backward hands and knees crawl for 5 minutes. Keep your head up with your eyes on the horizon, keep your lips shut, and maintain diaphragmatic breathing.

2) Forward Leopard Crawl for 5 minutes. Crawl on your hands and feet, keep your butt down below your head, keep your head up with your eyes on the horizon, keep your lips shut, and maintain diaphragmatic breathing.

Simply rest if (when) the mouth is opened, and nasal breathing can no longer be maintained. But, if you stop to rest, stop your clock. When you have recovered, resume the crawling and resume your clock.

If you tried this, you have done a great thing for both your nervous system and your diaphragm. Hopefully, you also understand how this adds a load to breathing. If you found these activities to be quite difficult, imagine how capable you, or your athletes, will become when these activities become as easy as checking your email on your smartphone. It can happen.

Maintaining diaphragmatic breathing under stress, exertion, and during work is the gateway to optimal human performance on and off the field, in sport and throughout life. It does build physical stamina, but it also lays the foundation for an amazingly resilient body that can weather the stresses of both sport and life. It also builds a mind that can maintain focus, clarity of thought, and enables best decision practices—all things essential to enhanced performance.

The point is, strengthen the taproot first. Develop the ability to breathe with the diaphragm during simple bodyweight, contra-lateral movements (practice forms of the gait pattern). Keep the head and gaze level with the horizon, and keep the lips shut and the tongue on the roof of the mouth. Crawling for time is one of the best ways to practice this. Once the body becomes proficient at maintaining diaphragmatic breathing through simple, low-stress contra-lateral movements, we can begin to strengthen the rest of the roots by adding load to gait pattern.

Loading the Gait Pattern

The gait pattern is the pattern that is designed to keep us strong and healthy by keeping the X tied together. When all four limbs work in coordination with their opposing counterparts, it nourishes the nervous system, maintaining or even restoring reflexive strength. Therefore, if we are loading the gait pattern to enhance the body's reflexive strength and further develop and strengthen the "roots of performance," we want to load the body in such a way that all four limbs are allowed to move according to their design. The best ways we have found to do this is by attaching a harness to the body and dragging a load, using packs and weight vests, or by attaching cuffs to the limbs themselves.

Whichever way the load is attached, the contra-lateral gait pattern must be maintained rhythmically and fluidly. Once the pattern breaks down, or if the limbs are restricted from their motion, the desired effect has been compromised and we have begun asking the body for something we do not want: compensation strategies.

The trick with adding load is not to cross the line of performance, the place where successful, desired performance turns into compensatory performance. We can load the body right to the edge of that line, though we don't necessarily have to, allowing the body to become accustomed to challenging loads over time. And, over time what was once challenging will become easy. This is how you push the line of performance further down the track and make the things that were once hard, easy. It's all about adaptation. This is where strength and performance can be enhanced, by developing an adaptive nervous system that is fast, accurate, responsive, and enduring.

Using a Harness

The safest place to start when adding load to the gait pattern is by using a harness. Because there is no load placed directly on the body itself, the body is never compromised due to fatigue or lack of concentration. If the person needs to stop and rest, they simply stop, and the pull being placed on their body stops as well. When the athlete is ready to move again, the resistance begins when they move.

Beyond safety, perhaps the best thing about attaching a harness to a person is that the pull of the harness feeds a reflexive response. When the head or torso encounter the pull of the resistance, the brain increases the neuro-muscular output to the body, and the athlete's posture becomes optimized to pull the load. The higher the harness is placed on the torso, the greater the reflexive response (or demand) is placed on the postural muscles. This is a fantastic way to develop optimal posture along with strong and enduring postural muscles. Optimal posture leads to optimal movement.

When adding a load, remember that the desired outcome is the same: the athlete should be able to maintain diaphragmatic breathing, the head should stay up, and the gait pattern should remain fluid. If any one of the Three Pillars is dropped, the athlete should rest, and the load should be lightened, if not removed. If the athlete can recover and continue while maintaining the Three Pillars, great. If not, it is time to rest and move on.

Coaching Moment

Build the capacity of all Three Pillars of Human Movement at the same time. Use the Pillars to know when to rest, back down, or move on. It's simple, really. If one of the Three Pillars breaks down, the line of desired performance has been crossed. This is where rest and load must be considered. Don't be so attached to the desired outcome of the training session that you miss what's happening in the moment of your athlete's training session. Outcomes are built in the moments. Be patient and allow your athlete's body to adapt. This is where you can really play a key role in your athlete's performance development.

Using Rucksacks and Weight Vests

Rucksacks and weight vests are also great ways to add a load to the body that still allow for fluid gait movement. Keep in mind that if the athlete is crawling, the load is now directly on their body. Unlike using a harness, if they stop to rest, they are still under load. Also, unlike the harness, when crawling, rucksacks and weight vests don't feed the same reflexive response. It is for this reason, in Original Strength, we prefer to load crawling with harnesses or other methods of dragging loads and not carrying loads.

Rucksacks and weight vests are great for loading marching and walking. Rucksacks do feed a reflexive response in the center of the body as the weight on the back wants to fold the athlete backward. This causes the abdominals to reflexively contract to keep the athlete upright. It doesn't really take much weight inside the rucksack to create this response. As little as 25 to 35 pounds is enough for a 200-pound man to develop his roots. More weight can be used as long as it doesn't cause any of the Three Pillars to collapse.

This is especially important when it comes to Pillar #2, activating the vestibular system—head control, in this case. The head must stay level with the horizon, over the shoulders. Placing too much load in the rucksack so that it causes "ruck neck" is crossing the line of performance. The head should not jut out well in front of the body because there is too much weight in the rucksack. Make sure the head remains over the shoulders and the athlete is moving with optimal posture. Another way you can help ensure optimal posture and fluid contra-lateral movement while rucking is to cinch the shoulder straps close together in front of the chest. This pulls the shoulder straps out of the brachial plexus and prevents discomfort and nerve issues in the shoulders and arms.

Weight vests don't feed a reflexive response like the rucksack, but they do stress the system by placing a load on the body. Carrying 20, 40, or 80 pounds of extra weight around for time and distance can significantly help develop the diaphragm's work capacity, which develops the entire body's work capacity. In truth, carrying any extra weight around for time and distance is a phenomenal way to build strength and work capacity in the body, especially with the Three Pillars in mind.

It should be mentioned that marching, walking, and hiking under load do offer one major advantage over crawling: they allow the arms to be freely driven from the shoulders so that the shoulders can achieve true extension. As wonderful as crawling is, it does not allow the shoulders to achieve the much-needed and nourishing extension of the arms extending back behind the body. Yes, the shoulders should swing the arms back behind the body. This may seem unusual in today's world of motionless arm walkers, but driving the arms from the shoulders to match the movement of the hips is the intended design to keep humans strong throughout life. And, just in case you have haven't noticed, our opposite limbs do, and are supposed to, mirror each other. That is, when the left hip goes into flexion, the right shoulder should go into flexion. When the left knee moves into flexion, the right elbow moves into flexion. When the left ankle dorsiflexes, the right wrist moves a small amount to mirror the ankle. In an unhindered gait pattern, the opposite limbs are mirrors of one another in rhythmic, fluid fashion. This can easily be seen in the freeze frame of someone marching or sprinting.

Loading the Limbs

Speaking of free-flowing limbs, the limbs can also be loaded to strengthen the roots of performance. Perhaps the easiest way to do this is to hold "Indian Clubs," or light, long sticks, such as dowel rods, in the hands when marching, rucking, walking, or even sprinting. The clubs do not have to be heavy. In fact, they should enhance the arm swing, not detract from it. It's the leverage that the clubs, or sticks, create through their length that enhances the arm swing. It makes the arm swing crisp and places an interesting demand on the center of the body, especially when speed is increased, like in a fast march. The length of the clubs also facilitates more shoulder extension. Keep in mind, if the clubs or sticks make the arm swing crisp, they also make the leg swing crisp as well. They mirror each other, right?

This is a must-try movement. Done for any length of time, this will be your athlete's favorite way to prep for movement or cool down from movement. But it can also be used as a training session on its own.

The limbs can also be loaded with crawling. Perhaps our favorite way to do this is by attaching a chain to the wrists and ankles by clipping a carabiner from the chain to an ankle strap with a D-ring attachment. Crawling while dragging a chain from the limbs is a powerful exercise that demands a huge reflexive response from the center of the X (the core muscles). This is another exercise that must be experienced to be understood. Simply watching someone do this will not mean much. You have to do it to know it and understand why you want others to do this as well.

When loading the limbs via chains, you can be creative. You can attach a chain to only the arms, only the legs, to all four limbs, to the opposite limbs, or to only one limb. But remember, the goal is to allow the opposite limbs to still move and flow together. If the load is too great, and the limbs can no longer maintain their contra-lateral pattern with each other, the desired effect is lost. The results can still be good, but we should strive for best and make sure the Three Pillars can be maintained.

The goal, with the movements we've listed, is to create a root system so deep, a nervous system so strong, that the athlete can freely and fully express their strength, speed, power, and skill, to fully optimize their ability to physically and mentally perform, while minimizing their risk of injury. These movements are RESETs to which we have added load. They are not easy. They demand a great deal of effort, in both mind and body. They nourish the nervous system while strengthening and tying the body together. They weave an X that is amazingly capable and resilient, ready to perform in life and sport for years to come. And that should always be the point of training.

4

THE TRUNK OF STRENGTH

"Night and day, while he's asleep or awake, the seed sprouts and grows, but he does not understand how it happens."

—Mark 4:27

In the previous chapter, I talked about loading the gait pattern to deepen and strengthen the roots of performance. The truth is, loading the gait pattern will also strengthen the body itself, or the "Trunk of Strength." In fact, it will make the body very strong. However, there is a limit to how much we can load the gait pattern and still honor the Three Pillars of Human Movement. Eventually, the free-flowing contra-lateral pattern will stop. And—this may be no surprise to you at all—having arms allows us to hold loads and manipulate loads greater than we otherwise could than by simply attaching a load to our bodies. If we want to develop greater strength, above and beyond the fantastic strength we can achieve by loading the gait pattern, then we need to implement ways to increase the load and or stress the body much further. Having a solid base of reflexive strength and control through loading the gait pattern allows us to do this with even greater returns, but most importantly, it allows us to do with a reduced risk of injury.

It should go without saying that efforts in strength training are meant to enhance the athlete and not undermine that athlete's health. But, even the best coach with the best strength training program will be limited by the athlete's nervous system. Adding too much load to an athlete who does not have a solid base of reflexive strength can increase the athlete's risks of injury. Adding too much training volume to an athlete, in the vein of strength training plus the demands of practice and skill training, without the athlete having the ability to recover, can also lead to increased risk of injury.

This is why it is so important to ensure the athlete owns their reflexive strength and they know how to Press RESET as well. Once a solid foundation of reflexive strength and control is established, efforts in strength training can become more effective and less detrimental. And, even if the volume of training is high, an athlete that is constantly Pressing RESET is an athlete that has the ability to recover quickly for the next challenge.

At its heart, the art of strength training is providing an appropriate load, or stimulus, to the body that creates the desired adaptive response: stronger, more powerful muscles. There are many methods of strength training, and all of them have their advantages. But, for the purpose of enhancing the overall health and performance of the athlete, we are going to focus on the whole athlete, mind and body. Keep in mind that nothing about the body is separated from itself. Physically demanding training is also mentally demanding. When done properly, training should enhance both the mind and the body together. A strong-minded, confident athlete, is an athlete who will rise to the occasion. In performance, everything matters.

Loading the X

To begin, we are going to look at strength training as if the body's opposite arms and legs were actually connected to each other—because they are. Remember, the body is an X. In this section, we are going to discuss intentionally contra-laterally loading the body's opposing limbs while strength training to strengthen their connection and intersection through the center. There are many movements that can be used to do this, but two movements that really stand out are cross-body single leg deadlifts (SLDLs) and getups.

The Cross-body Single Leg Deadlift (SLDL)

The cross-body SLDL is a fantastic movement for loading the posterior side (the back side) of the X. It connects the lats (latissimus dorsi) to the opposing glutes; it connects the wings to the wheels.

In the cross-body SLDL, the hand opposite from the stance leg grasps the weight that is to be pulled from the floor. For example, if you are standing on your right leg, you are holding the weight with your left hand. For some reason, this confuses about 90% of the population to whom I have ever tried to explain this. In the contra-lateral SLDL, performed as I just mentioned, the *unloaded* leg that reaches back is on the same side of the body as the hand that is holding the weight. This causes many to see this as performing the SLDL on the same side, or not contra-laterally. But again, that is the unloaded leg. I know I just wrote this above, but in an effort to deepen this into your nervous system, in the cross-body SLDL, if you are *loading* the right leg and *standing on* the right leg, the weight should be held in the left hand. Got it?

This seemingly simple movement is a great feat of stability, mobility, and strength. From a stability standpoint, the SLDL challenges the stability, or balance, of the stance leg as well as the rotational stability of the core. This is an anti-rotational movement or a "held rotational" movement. The weight being pulled from the floor is trying to break the position of the torso by placing an uneven demand on the posterior spinal stabilizers. And, because this movement is performed on a single leg, the body learns to stabilize the foot, ankle, knee, and hip against offset, uneven loads.

Did I mention that walking and running are done on a single leg at a time? Watch any athlete or human perform well when they move, and you will watch amazing grace and fluidity happen on one leg at a time, no matter how brief the moment. Stability, which does not mean static, motionless, or frozen, is dynamic. It is the dynamic fine-tuning of the stabilizers that hold the joints optimally for the body to perform the desired motion. When you challenge the body's stability in a familiar environment, the body learns and gives you more stability from which to move freely. I mentioned "in a familiar environment" because there are numerous ways to challenge stability. But, since life and most sports are typically played on solid ground, an air-filled device, slack-line, or cushioned mat may not be the best choices to challenge stability or upon which to strength-train. Unless, of course, those are familiar to your sport.

Having said all of that, the SLDL can be a very useful movement in strengthening the posterior side of the X from the center out or from the stabilizers to the movers.

The Getup

Is there a complimentary movement to the SLDL that works the anterior or front side of the X? Well, yes. The getup does that—sort of. There are many ways to perform a getup, but for understanding how the getup contra-laterally loads the X, we will discuss the Turkish Getup (TGU). Keep in mind that sandbag getups are also a phenomenal movement with very similar benefits, as are bodyweight getups (simply getting up and down from the floor).

In the traditional TGU, a weight is held in a fixed arm perpendicular to the ground while lying on the back. Then, through a series of movements, the person will stand while maintaining the fixed arm and its perpendicular relationship to the ground. In doing so, the opposing leg takes on much of the load throughout the transitions to standing.

The getup loads the front side of the X, and it makes a great complement to the SLDL. But to be honest, the TGU works *all* sides of the X. To get to this position requires a roll, challenging the anterior side of the X from the right shoulder to the left hip while challenging the posterior side of the X from the left lat to the right glute.

In these two unloaded, slightly exaggerated getups, it is easy to see how the other opposite limbs are contra-laterally loaded. This movement is a great way to contra-laterally load and connect the entire body. It also places an awkward load on the body resulting in a goofy type of strength. And this is perhaps the greatest thing about the getup in any of its forms. It challenges the body to move through transitions from lying to standing with or without awkward, imbalanced loads.

It's in moving through transitions and managing awkward loads that true strength is built, a strength that flows through all movements of a completely connected body, rather than trained isolated movements of a segregated body, enabling unhindered performance.

Ok, that last sentence was a mouth full, if not a mind full. Let me explain.

True Strength Vs Pretty Muscles

My eyes were opened to understand true strength when I was a firefighter. You might say I was "baptized by fire." Firefighters are professional athletes; the sport is just a bit different with larger consequences. In the fire department where I was employed, we had some pretty good physical specimens, men who looked like they could have been carved out of stone. They were muscular and powerful looking. We also had some "good ole boys" in the department; men with guts and a great deal of cushion. Looking at these men with cushion, you wouldn't necessarily think *fireman* or *professional athlete*. Until a fire happened.

When the bell hit and there was a fire to be put out, there was always a sharp contrast between looks and performance. The "good ole boys" could outlast and outwork the Atlas-looking boys every single time. It was amazing. What I learned from those incidents is that time spent in the weight room does not equate with performance or ability outside of the weight room. Seemingly so, in my department, time spent building "pretty muscles" actually took away from performance. And the guys, and gals who spent no time at all in the weight room but all their time working on their days off as farmers, painters, landscapers, etc., were the guys who could perform the most demanding physical tasks in moments of intense action and stress.

Please don't get me wrong, I'm not saying time spent in the weight room is useless. I'm not saying anything like that at all. If anything, I'm suggesting that what you do in the weight room, and outside of the weight room, matters. Inside the weight room, the goal of performance *outside* of the weight room must be the main focus. Keep the goal the goal. Building muscle for show and building strength to get stronger in certain lifts and exercises should not be the goal—a measurement maybe, but not the goal. The goal is performance enhancement, life enhancement.

Watching the performance of my granite-built fire brothers was eye-opening. But more sobering was the performance of my non-traditionally-strength-trained brothers, the off-duty farmers, painters, and landscapers. The firemen who engaged in manual labor—moving, manipulating, and shifting awkward loads with their bodies on a regular basis—these guys had real-world strength that allowed them to perform amazingly demanding physical tasks. And that is the real lesson; the body is designed to move in natural ways in a natural world to get things done. Natural human movements, manipulating awkward, heavy, difficult-shaped objects from one place to another is where true strength is born, and unhindered performance is found. Pretty muscles are just pretty. But true strength, or "old man strength," gets things done.

Speaking of old man strength, just in case you cannot relate to my fire department experience, my dad hung drywall for thirty years. Eight hours or more a day, five days a week, for about fifty weeks a year, for thirty years, my dad manipulated 100-pound boards of drywall all day long. I, on the other hand, spent my entire teens, twenties, and most of my thirties in a weight room. Don't worry. I have since recovered from that illness.

My dad is now almost 70, but to this day, I would never want to wrestle my dad or let him grab hold of me. I would lose quicker than I can blink, and I fancy myself fairly well-tied-together too—at least I do now. The point is that my dad built a deep-rooted, *real* type of strength, the kind of strength that allows you to perform well in life. He built this through a consistent life of managing awkward loads. The strength I built in the first 25 years of my strength training was built in a controlled weight room full of symmetrical, balanced loads. My weight-room strength never held a candle to dad's real-world strength. He is one of the strongest people I know outside of the weight room. He has old man strength. His muscles are not pretty, they're just full of stamina, strength, and power, and they get things done.

Building Old Man Strength for Optimal Performance

I'm not sure that future generations will have terms like *old man strength*. The more society progresses, and the more technology advances, the population of true laborers may take a sharp decline. Old man strength is generally built from working, from consistent, daily, physical labor. Occupations like construction and farming typically produce people with amazing work capacity and strength. The human body is indeed made to move, and it is also made to work. Humans can really get a lot of work done. If you doubt that, look at the ancient pyramids in Egypt, the temples in South America, or the beautiful architecture in Rome.

Can you imagine building pyramids in a world with no machines, but using only strong backs, powerful legs, and maybe a few horses and camels? I'm certain that the people of those times were physically capable of almost anything. Their architecture certainly suggests that, as does their art. I don't recall seeing many statues, sculptures, or hieroglyphics of the ancient times representing any human body less than athletic looking. Earlier man was strong and able. They spent hours a day on their feet, walking, hunting, building, moving objects, training for combat, farming fields, and so on. They were capable because they moved from one place to another and they manipulated the world around them. They used their body, all of it, as a whole unit, in a world where nothing was symmetrical or balanced except for the things they built.

Manipulating the world around you, learning to force your will and teach your body to move awkward objects—that is where real performance enhancing strength is built. In sport, on the field of play, the most awkward object an athlete will encounter, and the most common, is another athlete. To be strong enough and resilient enough to mitigate the challenges another moving, shifting, unbalanced body places on your body, you need to prepare your body by challenging it with awkward loads that would try to move you off balance. Symmetry and balance is perhaps one of the biggest traps of the weight room.

In the weight room, bars and dumbbells are easy to hold. They are built so they can be easily gripped. They are also built with precision to be balanced. Even kettlebells have a handle designed to allow you to manipulate it easily. Humans are clever. We have created a method of strength training by using tools (weights, machines, dumbbells, whatever) we have designed to allow us to have our way with them.

Now, don't get me wrong. Some more progressive-thinking coaches and trainers have realized the error in this, so they use things like sandbags, or long, weighted cylinders with handles to make the manipulation of these tools a bit easier. Now, don't get irritated, and don't throw your handlebars out of the weight room. They are still very useful tools. I'm only trying to get your mind opened to the fact that unless you're riding two-wheeled cycles for your sport, there aren't too many handles out there. So, spending all your time strength training on things that are easy to hold or things that are balanced could end up building a strength that is truly only useful when you're inside the weight room. Outside the weight room, life moves. It pushes you and tries to knock you off balance.

This brings me to another trap inside the weight room, rooting. What are your favorite exercises? Deadlifts? Squats? Bench? The snatch? Power cleans? They are all great. They all ooze strength and power. And, they are all static movements, in one spot, with feet generally symmetrically rooted into the ground. With traditional means of strength training, which have merit, we typically take up one spot of floor and wedge the body between the bar and the floor. We place all our force and power perfectly perpendicular to the ground. This does make the body stronger, specifically at doing such tasks, which is great if your sport is powerlifting or Olympic lifting. But again, in life and sport, athletes move across the field or across the court. They move their bodies into or from other bodies. They inflict force and they absorb force, from most all vectors imaginable, except those that run perpendicular to the ground.

This is why developing old man strength is so important. Can we just call old man strength *supercharged reflexive strength*? Because that is what it is. It is strength built on a solid foundation of reflexive strength through doing what the body was truly designed to do: Move from point A to point B. Moving from one spot to another, covering ground, with or without an object, that's the design. Just like loading the gait pattern strengthens and deepens the foundation of reflexive strength, moving asymmetrical objects or awkward loads from one spot to another, challenges the body in unusual ways and adds a more seasoned type of reflexive strength to the body; it reflexively hardens and fortifies the body, making it more capable and more injury resistant.

For example, we can use off-centered loads, or even shifting dynamic loads, to pull on the body and take advantage of the body's reflexive reactions (reflexive strength) to strengthen the body's stabilizers and decrease the body's reaction time. The stronger and more efficient the stabilizers, the faster the body can react, pro-act, and adjust, the stronger the body and the better the body can move. Off-centered loads, awkward and shifting loads, demand a reflexive response much like loading the gait pattern via a harness does. The right amount of pull, or challenge, results in the brain providing a greater output of neuro-muscular effort. This is a great way to build subconscious, reflexive strength that enhances overall strength.

Before I go any further, please understand, I'm not against traditional weight-room strength training. It offers many benefits and can be useful for developing hypertrophy, or "body armor," as Dan John calls it, and it can be used to develop strength in athletes. But, what I am saying is that the traditional method of strength training, while useful, may be lacking when it comes to optimizing athletic performance potential. Just know that there is more to building strength than a lifetime spent in a weight room will ever reveal, unless of course the objects in the weight room begin to be used to load the body asymmetrically and become treated as if they need to be moved from one place to another. You know, treating the inside of the weight room as if it were the outside world. Anyway, hang in there with me. If you love deadlifts, squats, the bench press, and the Olympic lifts, it's going to be okay. I promise.

Heavy Carry Day!

> "I consider that every general program to enhance athleticism needs a carry task." – Stuart McGill, Professor of Spine Biomechanics, University of Waterloo

Perhaps the simplest and most effective way to build this old man strength is to engage in regular carries. I was first exposed to carries by the two major influences and training geniuses in my strength training pedigree: John Brookfield and Dan John. Both exposed me to the value of carries at roughly the same time, so I guess I took notice.

John Brookfield taught me how to use carries to become uncomfortable and "relax in the distress." Carrying heavy loads for long periods of time is hard on the body, but it also plays mental havoc on the mind. It makes you want to tap out. In other words, John taught me how to make hard things easy by becoming comfortable with things that suck, like carrying objects for time or while covering set distances.

I once heard Dan say, "Doing the things you don't do makes you stronger." Dan was talking about his five fundamental human movements: push, pull, squat, hinge, and carry. He told several stories about how the athletes he trained became stronger when they engaged in the one fundamental movement they weren't doing. Now, either I heard Dan wrong, or I heard what I needed to hear, but every story Dan told that day was about an athlete getting stronger once they started performing carries in their training. What I heard Dan say was, "If you want to get stronger, do carries."

Later, as I got into Original Strength, and started thinking about the design of the body, it dawned on me; the body is made to walk. This helped me to really "enjoy" the fruits of heavy carries. I began carrying heavy objects for time and distance. What I learned is what I had already learned, but perhaps had not fully applied. John and Dan were right all along. Carries make you very strong, especially when layered on top of a deep root system established by Pressing RESET, like crawling for long periods of time or distance. Anyway, heavy carries can make you very strong because walking under load and with awkward loads develops the stability, mobility, and strength that is often missed in traditional strength training. It also prepares the muscles, tendons, joints, and bones for both sport and life.

Carries add another layer of strength to the trunk, truly making the body resilient. The list of ways to carry loads can probably not be exhausted if you have a healthy imagination. However, here are a few that develop tremendous old man strength:

- Any carry with a bottoms-up kettlebell. Holding a kettlebell upside down and walking with it is a great way to develop goofy strength. Reflexively, without thought, the body will adjust to balance the bell by firing muscles that can be near impossible, if not frustrating, to activate with conscious thought.

- Any overhead carry. If the athlete has the shoulder mobility, walking with anything overhead, even a symmetrical barbell, will build tremendous strength. Overhead carries alter the body's center of gravity, raising the center of gravity up towards the head. Babies build resilient strength because they learn to manage the heavy load of their head while they learn to stand and walk. Overhead carries can also offer similar advantages and gains in strength for athletes of any age. They are also great for enhancing shoulder stability and endurance. Whether using two hands, one hand, a balanced load, or an asymmetrical load, this is a powerful training tool. To explore how to develop old man strength, engage in asymmetrical loads overhead.

- Heavy suitcase, shoulder, or one-sided carries: Unilateral carries are fantastic for building core strength. As these carries also unbalance the body, they reflexively force the body to adjust so the torso does not tip or lean over. If the torso does lean too far, the load is either too heavy, the athlete doesn't have a great base of reflexive strength, or both. Otherwise, these carries build tremendous strength in the athletes' center, making their X very resilient.
- Heavy head carries: Making the head heavier, either by a head weight or a sandbag, and walking around, improves posture as well as it builds strong postural muscles. This simple exercise helps build great, fluid moving, healthy athletes.

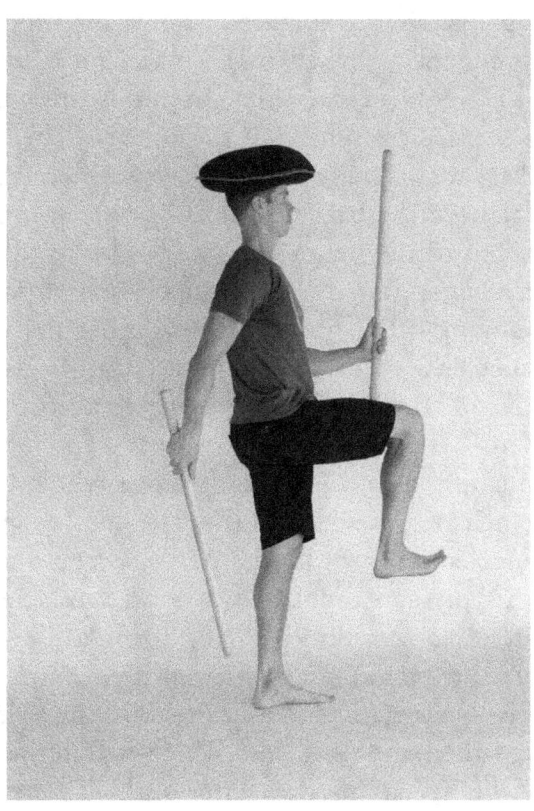

Manpower and Sleds

If I squint, sled work looks a lot like heavy carries to me. They both involve moving a heavy load from one place to another by walking, running, or crawling. The biggest and perhaps the best difference between training with a sled and performing heavy carries is that using a sled never places the body in any harm as the weight or load is never directly on the body. Because of this, sled work has a huge benefit to risk ratio. It's very low risk and high yield. It's not impossible to get injured by using a sled, but you've got to work at it. It is, however, impossible to not become stronger and more resilient by using a sled as a sled challenges the entire body in the realms of strength, stamina, and mental fortitude. It's very simple, but it's not very easy.

Almost every team or training facility has sleds, but that doesn't mean they use them for anything more than occasional "conditioning" (gassing or torture sessions) or employ them for their strength-enhancing benefits. This is a shame because pushing or pulling a sled requires the athlete to impose his will and body into moving the sled from point A to point B. Whether pushing or pulling, the athlete's body will intuitively and reflexively stack itself up to achieve the best positions and structure to get the job done. It's beautifully reflexive as well as beautifully effective. It teaches an athlete how to reflexively brace and position their bodies for moving other objects (think other players). It also teaches athletes how to brace for impact intuitively and safely impose their force into another athlete or absorb force from another athlete.

Again, pushing a sled is a tremendous whole-body effort. When the hands are pressed into the sled, they generate a great amount of mechano-receptor (the nerve sensors in the hands) input and this in turn reflexively fires the muscles throughout the entire torso. As the legs drive down and produce force into the ground, they, too, produce a reflexive muscular response throughout the lower body and the core. Pushing a sled connects the X through the hands and feet. This generates tension from both ends of the X, making the center of the X reflexively solid.

Similarly, but different, pulling a sled (think dragging backward) also generates tension through both ends of the X. The feet still push through the ground, but the hands are now being pulled against. This also generates a reflexive response from the body, stacking the spine by addressing the posterior side of the torso, and it teaches the shoulders how to stabilize when traction is applied to them (think gentle hanging).

Pushing a sled reflexively addresses the posterior side of the lower half of the body and the anterior side of the torso. Pulling a sled reflexively addresses the anterior side of the lower body and the posterior side of the torso. When both are included in a training regimen, the X is made stronger, and balance is achieved. Honestly, if a sled were all you had to strength train with, a sled would be all you need. It is the most undervalued and overlooked training tool you're probably not using. Just remember, when using a sled, friction/resistance, time, and distance are the name of the game. It's really not about the weight; it's about the work being done.

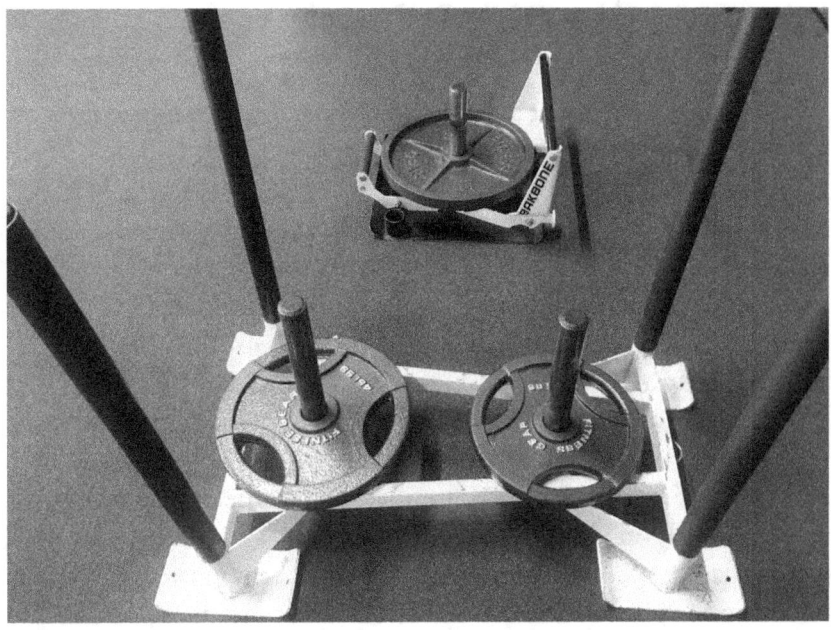

When Original Strength is present in an athlete, activities like pushing a sled or carrying an object for distance result in a subconscious, reflexive firing of muscles (reflexive strength) that generates optimal posture while performing the movement pattern. The body is designed to know how to brace, move, and support itself when, and before, it encounters resistance. The brain knows exactly how to align the vertebrae and position the limbs to create the right amount of force to move an object, or the body when an object encounters it. This is the essence of reflexive strength. Loading the gait pattern and carrying or pushing objects for distance is a simple way to increase this reflexive, goofy strength.

Note: Because carries and using the sled do not allow for all four limbs to freely move, we think it's a good idea to follow this type of training by "Pressing the RESET button" on your nervous system with a contra-lateral movement like crawling, marching, or skipping. The strength potential of the body flows from the movement design of the body. Constantly engaging in the gait pattern with all four limbs will keep the body strong and resilient.

WE WERE MADE TO MOVE

> "I praise you because I am uniquely and wonderfully made; your works are wonderful, this I know full well."
> —Psalm 139:14

This is true of each and everyone one of us. Isn't it encouraging? It is also true that we were made to move and meant to move. Movement builds our bodies, excites and soothes our minds, brings forth and settles our emotions, and connects us with others and our world. Movement takes us places and can lead us to accomplish great things. Excuse the pun, but movement *moves* us. Movement also nourishes our bodies, right down to the cellular level. Movement helps us to grow and express who we are. In essence, movement on all levels, no matter how great or limited (right now), plays a necessary and beautiful role in the fulfillment and expression of all of the wonderful qualities that God has poured into each one of us.

> "For you formed my inward parts; you knitted me together in my mother's womb."
>
> —Psalm 139:13

Move More, Move Better[5]

To nurture our growth and to fulfill all that we were meant to be, we must *move more!* Accomplished ultra-marathoner and OS Certified Pro, Sarah Scozzaro, said it this way: "Move as much as you can, as often as you can, in as many ways as you can." This applies to our everyday lives in the way we interact with family and friends, how we do our jobs, and how we spend our free time. Movement is perhaps the greatest vehicle for getting us to experience our lives. It makes everything better and richer. Yet, we now find ourselves in a modern world where we willingly or unwillingly forgo movement in favor of a sedentary lifestyle—so much so that we now have to train movement, the one gift we were preprogrammed with.

Here's the truth, movement was never meant to be relegated to a training session. Yes, we can train to improve or fine-tune movement, but each of us was created to be movement experts full of grace, strength, and power. But this doesn't appear to be the case in our modern world. Now, within a typical day, we may carve out deliberate time that we devote to movement. Some call this scheduled time a "workout" or "exercise". Perhaps my favorite of the terms used nowadays is "movement practice," denoting a specific time dedicated to the rehearsal of selected movement skills. Again, for the individual who goes to the gym or to an athlete in a team facility, it's just commonly known as "training."

Regardless of what you call it, it is very common and necessary to have dedicated movement practice in today's world. We simply just don't move as often as we were designed to move. We all have our own individual relationship with movement and a history that has led us to where we are now. We may have favorite movements or activities that we enjoy engaging in and that make us feel good. We may also have some movement limitations that we bump into on occasion. The exercises we know and do, the way we organize them, our opinions on training based upon our own experience and what others have taught us, are all a part of our movement history.

The exciting challenge and opportunity that lies ahead for you will be to see your movement and that of the individuals under your care (students, athletes, and clients), through the lens of Original Strength. If your goal is to improve your performance, to become more aware of your habitual movement within the broader scale of everyday life, or if you've carved out forty-five minutes of a busy day to workout, the concepts that Original Strength is built upon can, and will, help draw out the strength and the amazing qualities that are hidden inside each and every one of us. I believe Original Strength can maximize our potential and help us optimize the expression of our divine gifts.

To bring things into focus and guide our movement training with OS vision, Tim Anderson provided this inspired definition:

"Strength is mobility. Strength is stability. Strength is fast and slow. Strength is cardiovascular and muscular. All of those qualities of strength are really different sides of the same thing. And if one is lacking, they are all lacking."

The Major Human Movement Patterns

A common thread that is woven throughout Original Strength is the belief that the human body is truly wonderfully made. In Original Strength, we teach that our intricately constructed and complex bodies were built to be resilient and meet almost any challenge set before us. We are limitless in our creative potential and physical expression. Think of it, our ability to express ourselves in thought and movement are endless, without end. That said, it may be helpful to titrate human movement into basic categories that allow us to plan our movement training more efficiently. We can do this by viewing the major human movements through the lens of Original Strength. By doing this, we can take our programming to another level and enrich the movement of our athletes and ourselves.

In his 2011 book, *Intervention*[6], it was coach and author, Dan John, who beautifully separated human movement into to five basic categories for the purpose of simplifying exercise programming. Dan's Five Fundamental Movements include:

1. Pull
2. Push
3. Hinge
4. Squat
5. Loaded carry

Dan's approach is simple and ingenious. Yes, through the history of strength training, others have written about the need to deadlift, squat, press, pull, and carry heavy things; that's nothing new. But, Dan's approach and the discussions I've had with him have been a catalyst for change in my thoughts on programming. Dan "gets it." His approach is organized, balanced, effective, and it's particularly well-suited for athletes or those individuals focused on a more traditional view of gym-based fitness training. As much as I love Dan's approach, I now believe we can build upon it and amplify the traditional movements by Pressing RESET. By filtering our training through the concepts of Original Strength, we can enrich the response and *move better!*

In OS Performance, we expand the list of *Major Human Movements* to include *Six Purposeful Patterns*; movements that are loadable and trainable. These movements are important to our development and are a part of our daily lives; they may be progressed and regressed. Restoring, strengthening, and sustaining these basic movements is foundational to enhancing athletic performance and enriching our daily lives:

1. **Hinge:** Hip dominant, posterior emphasis, extension pattern; locomotion, jumping

2. **Squat:** Knee dominant, anterior emphasis, flexion pattern at ankles, knees, and hips; level changing
3. **Pull:** Posterior emphasis, shoulder extension, and elbow flexion pattern; drawing near
4. **Push:** Anterior emphasis, extension pattern; adding distance, creating space
5. **Gait:** Contralateral pattern with extension, flexion, and rotation, "ties us together" and gets us places
6. **Rotate:** Disassociation of the hips and shoulders, turning on an axis, crossing the mid-line.

These movement patterns were a part of our development from belly-bound infant to locomotive grown-up. They are exhibited in our daily lives, and historically, training within these categories has been the foundation of traditional progressive resistance exercise programs. Because of their importance in life and performance, these six purposeful patterns provide a practical starting point to create our Movement Grid. The grid is a flowchart that ties the RESETs together with the hinge, squat, push, pull, gait, and rotation. These major movements are listed along the x-axis (horizontal) at the top of the grid (see chart below). Along the y-axis (vertical) at the left margin of the page, there are five color-coded sections, each representing a different movement goal. These goals lead the way through a progression from preparation to performance that may be followed over a pre-determined block of training or worked through within a single workout session. The proposed progression for movement flows through the following groups:

1. Press RESET
2. Pattern the movement and establish competency
3. Tie the X Together
4. Build structure with strength & hypertrophy
5. Perform – add speed and power

ORIGINAL STRENGTH PERFORMANCE

	SQUAT	PULL	GAIT	ROTATE	HINGE	PUSH
RESET	Breathe; Supine Head Nods; Dead Bug; Half Rolls; Windshield Wipers; Rocking with Feet Dorsiflexed; Lego Rocking	Breathe; Supine Neck Nods; Prone Neck Rotations; Half Rolls; Commando Rocks	Breathe; Head Nods and Rotations; Segmental Rolls; Dead Bug; Speed Skater; Crawling; Cross-Crawls	Breathe; Head Nods and Rotations; Half Rolls from prone & supine; Windshield Wipers; Advanced Windshield Wipers; Frog Rolls	Breathe; Head Nods; Scary Baby Rolls; Half Rolls; 4-Point Rocking; Bird Dog; Crawling	Breathe; Head Nods in Plank; Extended Commando Rocking; Bird Dogs; Backward Crawling
PATTERN	TRX Squat; Strap Supported Squat; Face the Wall Squat; Goblet Squat; Sandbag Bear Hug Squat	Pull-Aparts; Face-Pulls; TRX Y-T-W-I Drills; Bat Wings	March with Load to: Head, Hands, Torso, Combo	Standing Roll; TRX "Rainbow" Stretch; TRX Windmill; KB Windmill	Hip Bridge; Toe Touch Drill; Touch the Wall Drill; Waiter's Bow	Standard Push-Up; OS Push-Up; Dive Bomber Push-Up
TIE THE X	Bear Hug Carry Overhead Squat; TRX Pistols; Split Stance Squat; Step-Ups *(Contra-Laterally Loaded)*; Lunges in multiple planes	Standing One Arm Row *(Double & Single Leg Stance)*; Renegade Row	Asymmetric Carries: -Suitcase -Bottoms Up -Racked -OH Waiter's Walk -Shouldering	Turkish Get-Ups; Sandbag Get-Ups; Chops & Lifts; Sledgehammer Strikes	Bottoms-Up Carry; Horn/Goblet Carry; Suitcase Deadlift; Single-leg Deadlift	Shoulder Tap Push-Up; Rolling Push-Ups; Standing One Arm Press; See-Saw Press; Landmine Press
BUILD	Leg Press; Machine Squat; Back Squat; Front Squat; Zercher Squat	Pull-Down; Pull-Up/Chin-Up; Chest Supported Row; Bent-Over Row; One Arm Row	Sled Push; Sled Drag; Wheelbarrow Walk; Carries: -Crucifix -Overhead -Rack -Farmer's	Jammer Rotations; Cable Chops and Lifts; Landmine Twists	45° Back Extension; Reverse Hypers; Glute-Ham Raise; Hip Thrust; Romanian Deadlifts; Regular Deadlifts	Shoulder Press; Incline Press; Bench Press; Decline Press
PERFORM	Squat Thrust; Jump Squat	Chest Supported Row; TRX Row; Standing Cable Row; Standing Band Row *(All at Speed)*	Skips & Bounds; Hill Sprints; Sled Push; Sled Pull	Med Ball Rotational Throw; Sledge Hammer Strikes	Jumps; Throws; Clean and Snatch	Explosive Push-Up; Med Ball Chest Pass; Speed Bench Press; Push Press; Push Jerk

© Original Strength Systems 2018

Color version of Human Movement Grid available at https://originalstrength.net/performance-grid.

Please note that the movement names in this grid may not be familiar to you. This is nomenclature that I use in my training world, but don't get caught up in the names. This is only meant to be an example of how I categorize movement.

Below are general goals for each level of progression:

Press RESET

- Pressing RESET restores reflexive strength, mobility, and stability. This is foundational to optimal human movement, and of course, athletic performance.

- It stimulates and refreshes the nervous system and activates the muscles for specific exercises that will be performed.

- It encourages full joint range of motion and facilitates learning of multi-joint movements by establishing efficient neural patterns.

- Pressing RESET is a great way to evaluate or "check-in" with how an athlete is moving at any particular moment in training.

- Pressing RESET trains the X. It ties the body together and prepares it for adventure.

Pattern the Movement[7] – Establish Competency; "Learn It"

- This is where we rehearse and refine technique to reinforce correct movement.

- Here we use low load and controlled speed to increase the proficiency of the movements that will be used in training.

- Increased volume may also be programmed here to develop the muscular endurance necessary to improve the quality of a movement pattern or to sustain motor control to complete a specific movement task over a protracted period of time.

Tie the X - Establish Symmetry and Strengthen the Structure

- Tying the X is where we use loaded, single-limb movements, or contra-lateral movements in training to "connect" the hips & shoulders; this develops a reflexively strong center, promoting the efficient expression of movement generated forces, and with it, the ability to control rotation of the torso.
- This is where we try to make the athlete impervious to injury.

Build Out the Structure

- This is where we add "armor" to the athlete by adding external load via the use of a modality (Barbell, Kettlebell, Sandbag) that is appropriate for the orthopedic needs and training experience of the individual athlete.
  - In contact sports such as American football, increasing muscle mass & tissue tolerance through resistance exercise can add an extra layer of protection for the athlete. Training with the intent to build "Armor" may enhance the resilience of the athlete, helping them better withstand the impact forces that are generated and received.
- Here, load is increased progressively and systematically over time for the purpose of increasing strength, endurance, and hypertrophy.

Perform – Produce Speed and Power

- Once competency in the movement is demonstrated by the athlete (i.e., they have gained sufficient strength, and their technique is "dialed in"), we add speed to movement.

- The goal is to select the appropriate movement and load to develop the biomotor abilities of speed and power which can then be applied to specific sports skills on the field or court.

Prepare to Train and Train to Perform

The OS Movement Grid provides another application of the example of the "Tree of Human Expression." Remember, the roots of the tree represent the nervous system. In the Movement Grid, selected Original Strength RESETs are associated with each of the Major Human Movement Patterns to nourish the roots and develop reflexive strength. Next, we then rehearse or pattern the major human movements. We then load the pattern and train the X to promote the growth of a big strong, trunk—our bodies. When the roots are deep, and the trunk is strong and stable, and the movements are skilled, then we are able to fully express the power that lies within us in any physical endeavor we choose. This holds true for every individual, over the course of an "active" lifetime. It can be applied to the long-term athletic development plan for an athlete, a specific phase of training within the yearly program for a team, or even condensed to draw more out of one single training day.

The Crux of the Matter

The truth is, the Human Movement Grid is one way to organize movements and represents the relationship between the OS RESETs and traditional exercise movements. Certain RESETs may unlock your potential for performance in a given exercise, while the impact of others may not be as significant. Hopefully, this opens a new line of thinking, leading you to consider creative ways to promote better movement and performance. The most thorough progression will begin with Pressing RESET and flow through all levels, including the addition of speed in the more technical movements of performance. Not all your clients or athletes will be able to or need to progress to this point. No matter how far along the continuum one progresses, adding the RESETs alone will promote improved movement.

Having said all of that, if the Human Movement Grid I shared above seems too complex or a bit overwhelming, notice the sections that have been bolded to stand out. If the training of your athletes is focused heavily on the gait pattern and tying the X together, you will build athletes capable of performing well in most any arena. As we discussed earlier, loading the gait pattern and loading contra-lateral movements strengthens the nervous system and ties the body together. It makes the body able for anything.

More Things to Consider as You Grow

As you spend time Pressing RESET, you will gain a better feel for the positive change they can elicit on movement. Time spent performing the RESETSs yourself, or after observing your population using them, you'll see the impact they can have on joint mobility and stability, i.e., "reflexive strength". What you begin to see through the "lens of OS" can be layered into your decision-making process when prescribing a movement plan for your athletes and clients. Below are selected general movement categories and some recommendations for the RESETs, that when applied, may create positive adaptations; these are some of the specific RESETs I use in my own training and in the programs for my athlete. For your reference, most of these movements can be found on the Original Strength YouTube page:

T-SPINE MOBILITY AND STABILITY:
Diaphragmatic Breathing
Prone Head Nods and Rotations
Rolling – Head Roll, "Scary Baby" Roll, Upper-Body Half Rolls from prone and supine, Windshield Wiper, Advanced Windshield Wiper
Rocking – Commando Rocking, Circle Rocks
Crawling
Carries – Rack Carry, Waiter's Carry

HIP MOBILITY AND STABILITY:

Diaphragmatic Breathing
Rolling – Lower-Body Half Roll from prone and supine, Frog Roll
Rocking – Lego Rocking, Adductor Rocking, One Legged Rocking
Crawling
Cross-Crawls
All Carries

ANKLE MOBILITY AND STABILITY:

Diaphragmatic Breathing
Rocking – Plantar Flexed & Dorsi-Flexed Rocking in a variety of foot positions, One Legged Rocking, keeping the ball of the foot of the extended leg on the ground, Lego Rocking
Crawling

ROTARY AND STABILITY:

Diaphragmatic Breathing
Rolling –Segmental Rolls, Frog Rolls, Elevated Rolls
Rocking – 4-Point Rocking, Bird-Dog Rocking, One Legged Rocking & One Arm Rocking
Dead-Bug, Gait Bug
Bird-Dog, Speed Skater
Crawling
Carries – Suitcase Carry, Rack Carry, Bottom's Up Carry, Horn Carry, Bear-Hug Carry

As you can see, although individual RESETs can be added to improve the quality of specific movements, all of the RESETs will collectively impact the body and its movement positively. Diaphragmatic Breathing, Head Nods, Rolling, Rocking, and Crawling all interact with each other. The total sum of the effects of all of the various progressions and regressions of the OS RESETs is greater than the individual parts.

Here are some examples of how to progress through the movement goals, pairing OS RESETs with some traditional exercises.

DEADLIFT

Press RESET:
Diaphragmatic Breathing in prone position x 20 breaths
Head Nods in prone position, resting on elbows and forearms, or
Head Nods in "push-up extended" position x 10 reps
Lower Body Half Rolls from prone position, or
Frog Rolls x 5 Rolls each direction
4-Point Rocking on Hands & Feet x 15 reps
Cross-Crawls x 20 reps

Pattern the Movement:
2-Legged Hip Bridges x 10 reps; 1-3 sets as needed

Tie the "X":
KB Bottom's Up Carries – *Pick up the kettlebell and hold it upside down in one hand. Carry it 10 yards. Put the bell down, switch hands and repeat.*

Between Work Sets:
4-Point Rocking x 10 reps
Marching (Cross-Crawls) x 20 steps

OLYMPIC LIFTS (SNATCH & CLEAN)

Press RESET:
Breathing in Commando Rocking position x 20 breaths
Windshield Wipers x 10 rotations
4-Point Rocking on hands & feet x 10 reps; Slow going forward, at speed moving back.
Backwards Crawling with load placed on head via the Original Strength Loop Harness x 20 steps.

Pattern the Movement:
Waiter's Bow (Hug Plate to Chest) x 10 reps

Tie the "X":
1-Leg RDL's with one Kettlebell in opposing hand from standing leg x 5 reps, R & L; 3-5 sets, add weight as needed

Between Work Sets, Press RESET:
Head Nods in 6-point position x 10 reps
6-point Rocking with toes dorsi-flexed <u>at speed</u> x 15 reps

SQUAT
Press RESET:
Diaphragmatic Breathing in "Crocodile" position x 20 breaths
Head Nods in supine-lying position (Chin Tucks & Flexion) x 10 reps
Dead Bug (tail bone off floor) - especially for Front Squats x 20 total reps
Upper Body Half Rolls from supine position x 5 each direction
Lego Rocking x 20 reps each
March in Place x 20 Reps

Pattern the Movement:
KB Goblet Squats x 5 reps; 3-5 sets, add weight as needed

Tie the "X":
Sandbag Bear-Hug Carry – *Pick up the Bag, bear-hug it to your chest, carry it 10 yards. Put it down. Repeat.*

Between Work Sets, Press RESET:
6-Point Rocking with feet dorsi-flexed x 10 reps
Dead-Bug (tail-bone off floor) x 20 total reps

PRESSING
Press RESET:
Diaphragmatic Breathing in "Crocodile" position x 20 breaths
Head Nods & Rotations in prone-lying position, resting on elbows & forearms x 10
Upper Body Half Rolls from prone position x 5 each direction

Commando Rocking x 20 reps
Axis Crawling on hands & feet x 3-5 "circles" each direction

Pattern the Movement:
OS Push-Ups x 10

Tie the "X":
Landmine Press from Half-Kneel x 5 reps, R & L; 3-5 sets, add weight as needed

Between Work Sets, Press RESET:
Commando Rocking x 10 reps
Backwards Crawling with load placed on head via the Original Strength Loop Harness x 10 steps.

PULLING

Press RESET:
Diaphragmatic Breathing in "Crocodile" position x 20 breaths
Head Rotations in prone-lying position, resting on elbows & forearms x 10
Head Roll x 5 each way
Head Nods in supine-lying position (Chin Tucks & Flexion) x 10 reps
Upper Body Segmental Rolling from prone & supine positions x 5 each arm
Commando Rocking x 20 reps

Pattern the Movement:
Mini-Band Pull-Aparts x 15

Tie the "X":
TRX One-Arm, Standing Row x 5 reps, R & L; 3-5 sets

Between Work Sets, Press RESET:
Commando Rocking x 10 reps

SPRINTING

Press RESET:
Diaphragmatic Breathing in 6-point Rocking positions x 20 breaths
Head Nods in 6-point Rocking position x 15 reps
Frog Rolls x 3 reps each direction
6-Point Rocking with feet dorsi-flexed x 20 rocks
Lego Rocking x 10 reps each side
Cross-Crawls x 20 reps

Pattern the Movement:
Marching Cross-Crawls with fingers spread x 20 yards, walk back. Repeat x 3
A-Skips with fingers spread x 20 yards, walk back. Repeat x 3
Heel to Hamstring Runs with fingers spread x 20 yards, walk back. Repeat x 3

Tie the "X":
Spiderman Crawl x 24 "steps", walk back. Repeat.

Between Reps & Sets:
Speed Skaters (Dead-Bug in Gait pattern) x 20 reps total
Elbow to Knee Cross-Crawls x 20 reps, building from slow to fast
A-Skips with fingers spread x 20 steps, building from "light" to "force"

No matter how creative you get with programming the RESETs and pairing them with traditional exercises, remember that there are three criteria that must be met to restore reflexive strength: The Three Pillars of Human Movement. We cannot stress this enough. They form the foundation of the Original Strength System, and all three are addressed when we engage in the developmental movements that we call RESETs[8]:

1. Breathe using the Diaphram.

2. Activate the Vestibular system by leading with the eyes and moving the head.

3. Engage in Contra-Lateral or Mid-Line crossing patterns (the Gait pattern).

Please keep these three pillars in mind as you add the RESETs to your toolbox. You are only limited by your understanding and creativity when it comes to program design. Here are some general guidelines that may be helpful to consider:

- The RESETs can be performed as a stand-alone movement practice, in part or whole, at any point in the day. First thing in the morning, the RESETs will get your mind and body off to a great start. Before a workout, performing the RESETs will "trigger" the body's Reflexive Strength and move the muscles & joints through ranges of motion to enhance performance in training. Including RESETs in the cool-down phase of a workout will unwind tension and facilitate the recovery process.

- There are regressions/progressions that can be performed standing up or bolstered by an elevated surface to meet individual orthopedic needs or limitations. Anyone can Press RESET, they simply have to "start where they are."

- The RESETs themselves, are corrective by divine design (just as they are); they may also be included alongside other restorative exercises in your movement practice.

- The RESETs can be used in conjunction with patterning movements to build upon each other and amplify movement efficiency.

- Selected RESETs pair well with traditional strength exercises ("Build") on the front end to prepare the nervous system and target muscles for the subsequent sets; between sets, a smaller dose of the RESETs will restore the nervous system and aid recovery to continue training at an effective level.

- RESETs can be part of a bedtime ritual to relax the mind and body to prepare for sleep.

With all of the good things that the RESETs do for the body, and with all of the applications that are possible, Original Strength RESETs can and should be performed each day—in truth, multiple times each day. Remember, we are made to move, and we should be moving every single day. It's important for our health and the health of our athletes.

To quote Dan Gable, *3x NCAA Champion, Olympic Gold Medalist, Former Wrestling Coach at Iowa*

"If it's important, do it every day."

5

THE BRANCHES OF EXPRESSION

"He shall be like a tree planted by the rivers of water, that brings forth its fruit in its season, whose leaf also shall not wither; and whatever he does shall prosper."

—Psalm 1:3

When an athlete (or any person) has a healthy nervous system and a strong body deeply rooted in reflexive strength, he is able to express himself in potentially unlimited ways. Strength, mobility, fluidity, speed, power, endurance, strategy, cunning, focus, creativity, acuity—they are all at the athlete's disposal. But remember, in performance, everything matters. Another way to say this is that when it comes to a person's ability to express their full potential, everything, every variable, matters.

Physical conditioning and preparedness can only take a person so far. The state of a person's mind is also of great importance for the freedom of their expression. And the mind is like an onion: it has layers. These layers, the conscious and the subconscious mind, can both be influenced by many variables. Take movement for example. Movement can influence both layers and lift a person's conscious thoughts and their unconscious thoughts, actions, and emotions. Yes, movement can physically help a person feel and perform better, but it can also mentally help a person feel and perform better, giving them the capacity to think more clearly and make better decisions. Movement can remove barriers in the body and threats in the nervous system, threats that would hinder mental and physical performance. Again, there are many variables, internal and external, that can either improve or decrease athletic performance.

In the following sections, we are going to talk about the variables that affect the athlete's mind and the stressors they create. After all, if we want to improve and optimize an athlete's performance, we must address these threats, these stressors, because they ultimately influence the nervous system. Movement, emotions, the conscious and subconscious mind are highly intertwined. In fact, there is no separation inside of a human being. The being is the dance of everything about us and in us. Nothing is apart from itself. Everything about a person is layered and woven together to make the whole person. The outside, the inside, the physical, the mental, the emotional, the environment, the social, the belonging—they all come together and are interwoven to create the individual and the individual's expression.

When it comes to physical and mental expression, everything matters.

As a coach, you must become aware of all of the variables that affect your athlete. You must also become aware of the one thing you possess that can mitigate many of the internal stressors the athlete has. But first, let's discuss the often talked about and perhaps one of the most easily dismissed variables of performance: recovery.

Recovering to Perform

Much has been written about recovery over the years and nothing new will be written here. The fact is, if an athlete cannot recover from their training, their practice, their days, and their moments, they cannot optimally perform. Having the ability and the opportunity to recover from the stresses of their life is essential for them to be able to express themselves optimally.

As a coach, you have the greatest influence over recovery in the areas of training and practice. It's your job to oversee and program your athlete's training as well as their recovery. And as good as you might be in this area, there are still areas far out of your control, like the amount of sleep they get, the quality of sleep they get, the quality of nutrition they consume, and the way they generally handle the stresses of their "at home" lives. Even if those these other areas are further out of your span of control, you do still have influence that spills over into these areas.

For example, teaching an athlete how to Press RESET, can actually have a great carryover into how they sleep at night. I once met a starting linebacker for the Baltimore Ravens who slept through the night for the first time in eight years once he was taught how to breathe with his diaphragm. Can you imagine how an athlete's performance might improve if they were suddenly able to sleep restfully through the night after not having been able to in several years? Can you imagine how their home life and relationships might also improve? Speaking of sleep, did you know there appears to be a relationship between sleep deprivation and injuries in young athletes?[9] Not only does sleep affect performance, but it may also help lower the risk of injuries. Just in case you didn't know, adults should receive between 7 to 9 hours of sleep per night and teenagers should have between 8 to 10 hours of sleep. Be honest. Do you think your athletes get that much? Do you get that much? If you don't, how well are you performing?

Another crucial area of recovery that must be addressed is recovering from the moment. In a game, and often in life, events happen fast. "Good" decisions are made, and "bad" decisions are made. How an athlete processes these events and their thoughts around them will determine how they continue to play and perform. Some athletes can move on from a mistake or a loss unaffected and even use the mistake or loss for inspiration to rise to the next occasion. Others can't. The mistake or loss may remain in their head; it may eat their confidence; it may increase their stress and take them into flight mode, far beyond fight mode. It's odd. You can have two athletes both face the same event and for one athlete, it catapults them to a higher level, and for the other athlete, it tanks them, and they fall apart. What's the difference? Ultimately, the answers rest in their nervous systems.

Original Strength and the Nervous System: Optimizing Performance and Health

The nervous system rules all other systems. It is connected to every part of the human body via 43 pairs of nerves, 31 originating from the right and left side of the spine and 12 pairs going to and from the brain. It is divided (but still interconnected) into two subsystems, each of which is further divided into other subsystems concerned with various operations of the body. If we stretched out all of our nerves, they would stretch to an incredible 46 miles! The electrical impulses that carry information to and from our brain and spinal cord can travel at speeds up to 268 miles per hour. There is an estimated 95 to 100 billion nerve cells in our bodies and approximately 85 million of these are located in the human brain.

Our nervous system is tasked with coordinating everything we do. It regulates our heartbeat, our respiration, our hormones, our digestive system and our immune system. It gives infinite life to our expression of emotion, thought and physical movement. Indeed, our very existence and the quality of our lives depends on having a healthy nervous system. It is the one system that all other systems of the body depend upon and are interwoven with.

So how does Original Strength play a role in how our brain and body function? Is it possible to use the resets in Original Strength to benefit and improve performance? Can a system of training that focuses on the three pillars of human movement as its bedrock benefit athletes of all sports? Before we get into that, a broad and admittedly general overview of the nervous system may help you understand how Original Strength can play a critical role in human performance.

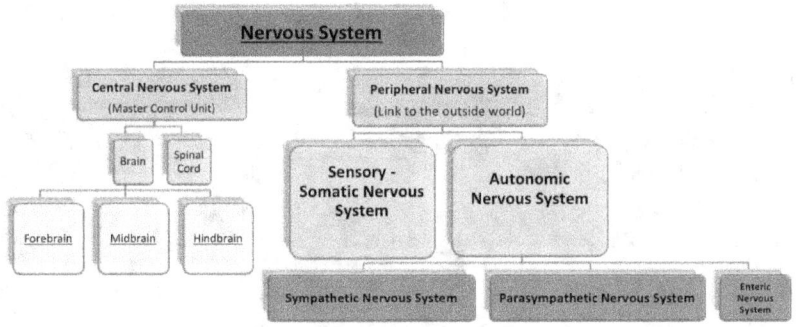

Figure 1

As mentioned above, the nervous system is divided into two main subsystems: the central and peripheral nervous systems. These two systems work in concert with one another to carry out the daily mundane, yet essential, components of life, in addition to the fantastic feats of athletic expression of which we are capable.

The Mundane

The Fantastic

The Central Nervous System

The central nervous system consists of the brain and spinal cord. The CNS serves as the master control unit and is responsible for most of the body's functions including:

- Awareness
- Movements
- Sensations
- Thoughts
- Speech and memory

The Brain

The brain is divided into three component parts: forebrain, midbrain, and hindbrain (see Figure 2). This follows the "triune brain" model proposed by physician and neuroscientist Paul D. MacLean in 1968 (further expounded upon in his 1990 book,

The Triune Brain in Evolution: Role in Paleocerebral Function). It might be helpful to think of the divisions of the brain as layers having a central core. The higher the layer, the more complex the functioning.

The forebrain is the "newest" layer of the brain and is also referred to as the neocortex. This region of the brain houses elements of living such as language, imagination, abstract thought, altruism, and consciousness. It is thought that the neocortex began its development in primates two to three million years ago. It has an almost unlimited capacity to learn and acquire new knowledge. In the triune model of the brain, it is thought of as the thinking portion of the brain.

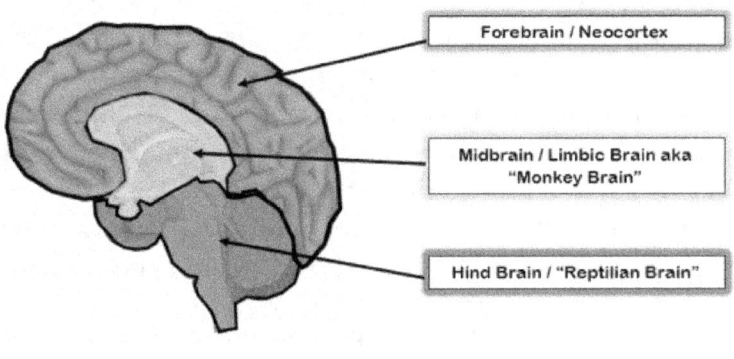

Figure 2

The next layer down is the midbrain, also known as the limbic brain. This portion of the brain first appeared in small mammals about 150 million years ago. The midbrain helps to regulate movement and aids in the processing of auditory and visual information. The midbrain/limbic brain includes the hippocampus, hypothalamus, basal ganglia, cingulate gyrus, and amygdala. The amygdala is the emotional center of the brain, while the hippocampus forms memories about past experiences. I would call it the "feely" or emotional portion of the brain.

The hindbrain, also known as the reptilian brain, is the oldest of the three evolutionary levels of the brain and first appeared in fish 500 million years ago, according to scientists who study this stuff. The hindbrain is referred to as the reptilian brain because this portion of our brains includes the main structures found in the brains of all reptiles. It is composed of the medulla, the pons, and the cerebellum. Together, these structures control and regulate what are called vital bodily functions such as breathing, heart rate, body temperature, and balance.

These three levels of the brain do not operate inside of a vacuum, independently of one another. Rather, they are all interconnected via neural pathways and serve to influence each other based on external and internal stimuli.

Spinal Cord

The second part of the central nervous system is the spinal cord. The primary function of the spinal cord is to act as a relay station between the brain and the body as well as to carry sensory information from the body back to the brain. In this capacity, it carries information gathered by the second major division of the nervous system, the peripheral nervous system, to the brain for analysis as well as motor commands from the brain out to the periphery of the body. Without it, the command and control center of the nervous system (the brain) would largely be unable to communicate with the rest of the body or interact with the outside environment.

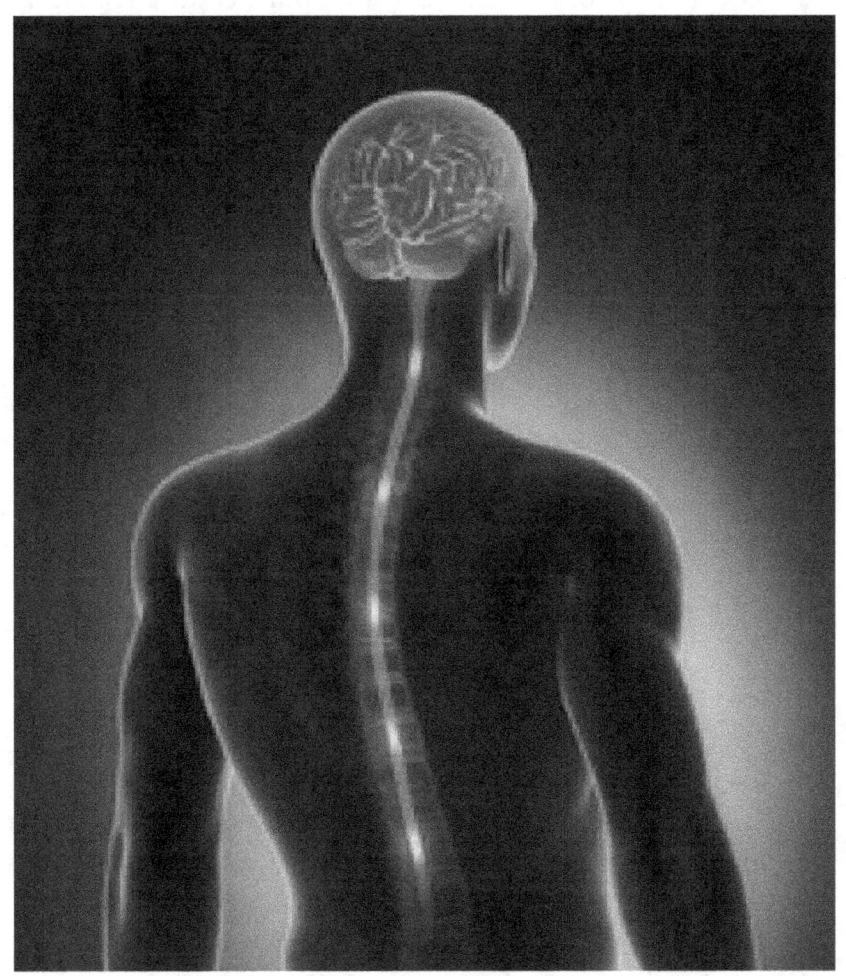

The CNS

The Peripheral Nervous System

The Peripheral Nervous System is our brain's link to the outside world. More accurately, it is the portion of the nervous system that exists outside of the brain and the spinal cord. The PNS is subdivided into the sensory-somatic and the autonomic nervous systems. Each of these systems controls movements of the body, but in distinctly different ways.

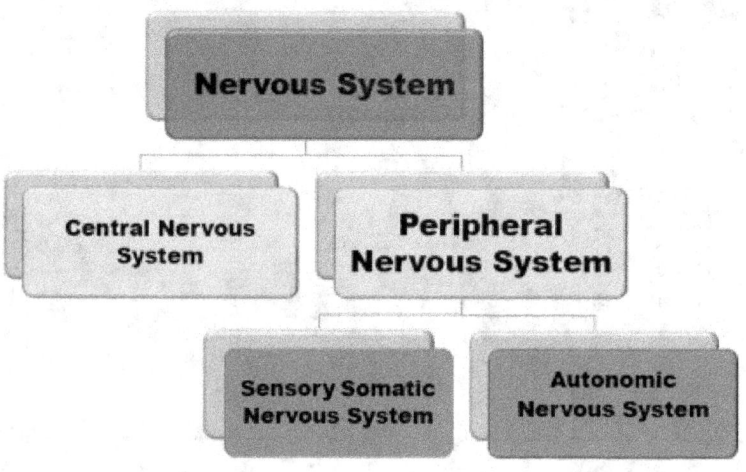

Figure 3

The Sensory-Somatic Nervous System

The sensory-somatic nervous system is primarily concerned with the conscious perception and control of movement. We receive information about the world from specialized receptor cells that are connected to sensory neurons. The type of information we receive depends on what type of receptor is activated:

- Pressure (mechanoreceptors)
- Pain (nociceptors)
- Temperature (thermoreceptors)
- Joint position and movement of muscles (proprioceptors)

This information is carried to the spinal column via a sensory nerve where the information is routed to the brain for further analysis. Stated another way, we gather information about the outside world, route it to the brain, and then make an action via a motor command on how to move/respond to that information. (See Figure 4)

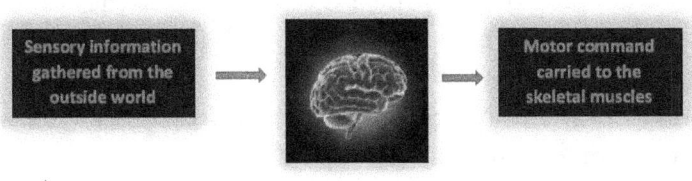

Figure 4

The information we receive in our brain is both conscious and unconscious, though we are mostly not aware of this transaction. It is estimated that of the 400 million to 2 trillion bits of sensory information arriving at the thalamus, only 4 to 2,000 bits are of the conscious variety. It is interesting to note that the thalamus processes that amount of information every second!

Original Strength plays a role in how well this aspect of the nervous system can function. To understand how this works, you'll first need to understand how the body divides up the tasks of synergistic muscles acting upon a joint(s) to create movement. To simplify, the body has two types of muscles (when it comes to movement):

1. Muscles that stabilize joints

2. Muscles that move joints

Before going any further, it is important to recognize that stability is not the absence of movement; it is the control of movement. Stability means, "The property of a body that causes it when disturbed from a condition of equilibrium or steady motion to develop forces or moments that restore the original condition."[10]

Think of it this way—if you stand on one foot and try to maintain balance, you will notice that the muscles and joints of your foot, ankle, knee, and hip are all moving. Or stated another way, they are making small corrections to maintain an upright posture and not fall. This is stability.

You need both stabilizers and movers, working together, to create efficient movement. Muscles that stabilize a joint are first to the movement party and the last ones to leave. They are easily activated and are fatigue resistant. They help to maintain posture and center the joint for optimal movement. They are dependent on sensory information gathered and processed at an unconscious level for optimal performance.

Muscles that move joints fire just a little slower than stabilizers, meaning they have a higher firing threshold, and in comparison, are easier to fatigue than their stabilizing counterparts. These muscles are largely dependent on the sensory-somatic nervous system for discharge. The "movement thought" needs to be created in the brain before they can fire. (Think of executing a biceps curl. You have to think about that for it to happen.) They are capable of extremely high levels of tension that can be used for expressions of speed, power, maximum strength, and endurance.

The lynchpin in all of this is the nervous system. Stabilizers receive their marching orders via the information received from sensory information that is routed from the environment through the vestibular system and into the brain for processing (see Figure 4). Once the information is processed, a motor pattern is automatically sent out to the appropriate stabilizing musculature at an unconscious level. From a movement perspective—and more specifically, a stability perspective—the information that the stabilizers need to perform optimally is determined by the quality of that neurologic information. If junk goes in, then junk goes out. The RESETs in Original Strength stimulate the vestibular system constantly, and they "clean up" the information going to the brain. They engage and stimulate the highly reflexive pathways of the deep core stabilizers:

- Diaphragm
- Pelvic floor musculature
- Transverse abdominals
- Multifidus muscles of the spine

The RESETs in Original Strength also stimulate joint stabilizing muscles of the periphery such as the shoulder's rotator cuff muscles, scapular stabilizers, and the deep stabilizers of the hip joint. If these pathways are not stimulated regularly, their effectiveness will become compromised and, in some cases, the ability to use them efficiently will be lost due to neural pruning (use it or lose it). The consequence of this is not lost upon the inherent wisdom of the body as it craves stability over mobility. If given a choice, the body will become more stable or hyper–stable (stiff or inflexible) in the absence of properly functioning stabilizers. The movers then have to take over the job of stabilizing in addition to doing their preferred job of moving joints. The result is inefficient, restricted, and sometimes painful movement. In a worst-case scenario, injury can occur as a chronically unstable joint placed under excessive load can compromise other tissues on the articulating joint surfaces, causing damage to the joint.

One of the principal benefits of Original Strength is that it takes the brakes off the prime movers by stimulating the reflexive joint stabilizers to do their job optimally. You need both of these classes of muscles working well together, in balance, to perform any type of athletic movement—or any movement, for that matter. This has massive implications for strength, power, and endurance performance. If the body is always fighting itself with one foot on the brake because of a perceived or real movement malignancy, injury is more likely, endurance is compromised, and strength and power levels become sub-optimal.

Think of this: Maybe the reason for a stagnant bench press or squat in the gym or a slow 40-yard dash time has nothing to do with desire, nothing to do with sets and rep schemes, and nothing to do with the frequency or timing of training. Maybe all the athlete needs to do is "Press RESET" on their nervous system more often. When the body is able to move the way it was intended and designed to move, it becomes easier to express its physical gifts and talents.

The Autonomic Nervous System

The autonomic nervous system is the other branch of the peripheral nervous system (see Figure 3). Its primary function is the unconscious regulation of smooth muscle tissue, such as the organs of the viscera and the heart. It also regulates blood circulation and respiration, as well as certain glands. The autonomic system functions reflexively and involuntarily, and we are typically unaware of its utility and effect on the body. The ANS is always on, even when we are asleep. It is the involuntary portion of the nervous system that serves to fine-tune automatic muscular responses and organ systems in direct accordance to stimuli it receives from the outside and internal environment.

The ANS is subdivided into the sympathetic nervous system (SNS), the parasympathetic nervous systems (PSNS), and the enteric nervous system.

THE ENTERIC NERVOUS SYSTEM

This portion of the autonomic nervous system governs the operations of the gastrointestinal tract. It is thought of as separate from the autonomic nervous system as it can act autonomously from the ANS. However, it is heavily innervated by the ANS and has the capacity to communicate to the CNS via the SNS and PSNS. To gain a comprehensive overview of the entire ANS, it is presented here.

The SNS and PSNS can be looked at as opposite or complementary divisions of the ANS. In many respects, when dominant over the other, each has mostly the opposite effect on the body that the other system has. Each of these branches of the ANS can be manipulated for performance—upregulated or down-regulated using the "Big 5" Original Strength RESETs and their own progressions and regressions.

THE SYMPATHETIC NERVOUS SYSTEM

Commonly known as the "fight, flight, or freeze" portion of the ANS, it is activated when our sensory systems detect stimuli that we interpret as threatening. In actual life or death situations, the SNS is invaluable. It heightens our strength, environmental awareness, and increases heart rate and blood flow to prepare us to either fight or flee. The drive to survive is a strong one and will dominate in times of real or imagined danger. All of the sensory system's information gathering ability is heightened, making us hyper-aware of our environment and getting us ready for action—all without any conscious thought. Researchers concluded that all different types of stressful stimuli have the same predictable effect on the body, which in turn reacts by activating the SNS to varying degrees.

Examples of stress types:

- High-intensity work
- Anticipation of events
- Arguments
- Becoming startled
- Loud, noisy environment

The response of the SNS is typically proportional to the perceived stress level. When we detect something that we believe to be inherently dangerous, we respond with an appropriate level of SNS arousal. Conversely, when we detect lower levels of threat, the SNS is activated at a reduced level in accordance with the threat. Physical, psychological, emotional, and environmental stress can all activate the SNS.

It's important to remember that human beings are all different and have different life experiences. These life experiences can have a dramatic effect on what we interpret as stress and how we deal with it. What is stressful to one person, may not be as stressful to others. This is evident to me on a personal level.

Brian, a friend of mine, served in the military and had no issues with jumping out of planes, swimming long distances in open water, or being crammed into tiny, dark, water-filled places (claustrophobia, anyone?).

I, on the other hand, do *not* do any of those things well. Even thinking about it freaks me out a bit. According to Brian, research was done on applicants for this particular job. The researchers wanted to know why some people were able to pass the selection process and others were not. One of the determining factors was how well applicants dealt with stressful stimuli. When presented with a stressful situation or circumstance, most had a similar stress response. However, the difference occurred in how quickly the successful applicants were able to deal with the stress and return to baseline levels versus the unsuccessful applicants. In other words, everyone got stressed, but those that could effectively deal with the stress quickly had a better chance of success in comparison to those that stayed in an elevated level of arousal. As individuals, coaches, therapists, etc., we should be sensitive to this nuance of training/rehab and take steps to mitigate its effects on those we are working with, so we can optimize performance.

As it relates to training, sports, and general competition, it is not uncommon for athletes to develop anxiety related to various aspects of sport. By relaxing the athlete first, and then exposing them to low levels of competition or aspects of the stressful stimuli, it is possible to overcome the anxiety that they feel. A warm-up using Original Strength strategies may be one of those methods that can be used in situations such as this. With an emphasis on deep diaphragmatic breathing, gentle rolling and rocking, Original Strength is very soothing to the brain and nervous system. In fact, it counteracts the SNS and upregulates the parasympathetic nervous system, the counterpart to the SNS. A look at the graphic on the following page will serve to underscore this narrative (Figure 5).

	Sympathetic NS	Parasympathetic NS
State of Function	Prepares body for action	Restore or maintain state of calm
Neural Pathways	Short pathways; fast system	Long pathways; slow system
Heart Rate	Speeds it up	Slows it down
Lungs	Dilates bronchial tubes and increases respiratory rate	Constricts bronchial tubes and decreases respiratory rate
Gastrointestinal System	Decreases gut motility and blood flow from GI	Increases stomach movement and secretions
Musculoskeletal System	Increases tone and blood flow to muscles of the extremities	Decreases muscular tone
Eyes	Pupils dilate	Pupils constrict
Salivary Glands	Decreases production of saliva	Increases production of saliva
Hormones	Increases adrenaline and cortisol (catabolic)	Increases growth hormone, DHEA, testosterone and estrogen (anabolic)
Body Temperature	Increases body temperature	Decreases body temperature
Activity	Naturally active during the day	Naturally active at night

Figure 5

Chronic stressful living can leave us in a constant sympathetic state, leading to a host of problems, such as an inability to concentrate, poor motor control, impaired posture, weight gain, inflammatory disease states, insulin resistance, speech pathologies, and sleep disorders, to name a few. When our body is in a state of perceived or actual stress, thus being driven more from the sympathetic nervous system, we don't have time to activate the neocortex of our brain (where higher-order thinking and complex decision-making occur), ponder the meaning of life and our place in this world. *The exact opposite of that tends to happen.*

When we go through life in a constant state of low-level SNS arousal, we are living in a perpetual state of low-level survival mode. Things irritate us more, we have a quick temper, and we are easily distracted and have difficulty with mental focus. We become sick more often and have greater difficulty recovering from illness. Research has found that chronic levels of psychological stress are also associated with the body losing its ability to regulate the inflammatory response, and as a consequence, leading to the development of disease. Bouncing back from workouts and competitions takes more time. We don't absorb nutrients from our diets, and we even become forgetful and absent-minded. Our ability to handle stress can have more than just performance benefits.

THE PARASYMPATHETIC NERVOUS SYSTEM

This is the counterbalance to the SNS, the "yin of the yang," if you will.

It is known as the "rest and digest" portion of the ANS. Under normal non-threatening conditions, we should be using this portion of the ANS for daily living. Under the influence of the PSNS is where greater learning and growth of our brains and bodies takes place. When we are in a state of PSNS dominance, we are able to access the higher functions of the brain in the frontal lobes that helps us learn complex new motor tasks, be more creative, as well develop emotional empathy, altruism, and love. The PSNS is anabolic and is responsible for nourishing the body, helping it to recover from different types of stress. Viewed through the lens of performance training, being able to access and manipulate this avenue of the autonomic nervous system is crucial for optimal growth and development.

If you think about it, people don't get stronger during a training session. To the contrary, they become more fatigued than when they started, their muscles feel weaker and cannot produce the same levels of force, and they get slower and less powerful. It is in the recovery phase, after they finish the workout or training session, that the real gains in performance are realized. Entering into the parasympathetic state is critical for optimal growth and recovery. In fact, our ability to recover from stress is directly related to our ability to utilize the parasympathetic nervous system.

To understand how Original Strength and the "Big 5" RESETs can help us get to this parasympathetic state faster, let's take a closer look at what is called the human stress response. With a better understanding of how our bodies react to stress, it will become easier for you to use the Original Strength RESETs to their fullest.

The Human Body's Stress Response

Everything that happens to us is merely an event. How we perceive the event, highlighted by emotion, determines whether the event is stressful or not. One man's stress may be another man's joy. It's a matter of perception. It can also be a matter of imagination. Because humans have the capacity for creativity and forethought, we can anticipate or imagine stress ahead of time before it even happens. This imagined stress is known as anxiety. Whether real or imagined, the physical response to stress and anxiety is the same.

When we encounter stress, we enter the sympathetic state, our body releases adrenaline and cortisol, and we go to "fight, flight, or freeze." This can be a great response if the release is appropriate to the actual stressor. After all, the sympathetic nervous system helps us to survive the threats of danger. But remember, stress can be imagined, interpreted, or perceived. How a person perceives the stress greatly influences the stress response. And, if a person is always under the weight of anxiety due to imagination or perceived life situation(s), then the person may always have adrenaline and cortisol flowing through their veins. This is not optimal to health and performance as there is no perpetual emergency.

Again, adrenaline and cortisol are very useful in an emergency. They help us to survive. But in a chronic state of stress, they do not allow us to thrive. Let's take a look at how they affect the body.

Adrenaline

Adrenaline increases heart rate, blood pressure, respiratory rate, and stroke volume. It dilates the pupils and moves the eyeballs peripherally. It shunts blood flow away from the gut and cerebral cortex of the brain and sends it to the peripheral muscles (arms and legs) to ready the body for action.

The increase in blood flow ensures a greater dispersal of electrolytes to the cell membranes of the muscles so they can contract. The increase in electrolyte dispersal also lowers the cell membrane potential from -70mv to -60mv or less. When the membrane potential drops, lower levels of stimuli are required to activate the defensive mechanisms of the body, thus making the body hypersensitive to all of the stimuli coming its way. While this is necessary for the survival mechanism, the reduced blood flow to the cerebral cortex and the hyper-awareness of all stimuli makes learning new tasks difficult and concentration on more than one thing next to impossible.

Stated another way, this part of the stress response is set up for one thing: moving the body immediately in response to the perceived threat. The dosage of adrenaline into the system is dependent on the perceived threat level. The right amount of adrenaline can be a great performance enhancer. Too much adrenaline can be a performance destroyer. It's a matter of balance in the autonomic nervous system.

Cortisol

Like adrenaline, cortisol can play both in a positive and negative way as it relates to human performance. The difference between the positive and negative effects of cortisol have everything to do with the length of time cortisol is being produced, an acute release versus chronic release.

In the acute release of cortisol, as a part of the stress response, the hormone will act to break down proteins into amino acids that are then released into the bloodstream, and from there, into the liver. In the liver, the amino acids are then converted into glucose (a process known as gluconeogenesis) for an immediate form of energy when our body needs it most.

Cortisol will also stimulate the release of fatty acids from fat cells by stimulating the release of another hormone called HSL (hormone-sensitive lipase). HSL is responsible for the breakdown of triglycerides into diglycerides, monoglycerides, and fatty acids. In other words, cortisol is responsible for the release of fatty acids into the bloodstream to be metabolized for energy. This is a good thing, especially when you need energy right away.

Cortisol has another positive benefit as it is also a part of the acute inflammatory response to injury. It is a powerful anti-inflammatory and keeps little bumps and bug bites from turning into massive lumps.

Cortisol's function is to primarily help us survive from emergent threats. Anything that is not directly involved with keeping you alive at the moment of threat is suppressed. Digestion, immune function, complex thinking, and reproduction are all non-essential in the moment of threat, and as a result, they are taken offline. This is a good thing. Until it's not . . . Cortisol can become a problem when the "cortisol faucet" is always dripping, and in some cases, running rampant, and we can't turn it off. When cortisol is chronically flowing into the bloodstream, its effects can be quite problematic.

Cortisol is catabolic, and it causes the loss of muscle tissue as a part of the gluconeogenesis process and therefore interferes with the process of regeneration and recovery after exercise. Cortisol can reduce protein uptake in cells by as much as 70%.[11] It also suppresses the immune system by decreasing white blood cell count, thus reducing antibody formation (B cells) as well as T cell formation, which is responsible for the adaptive immune response. Intense training also leads to immune system suppression. If we put these two stressors on the body at the same time, the result is fairly predictable: We become more susceptible to infection and disease.

Another issue with chronic cortisol release is that insulin sensitivity at the cellular level is decreased, and over time, the cells become more insulin resistant. Insulin sensitivity is a term used to describe the cells' ability to bond with insulin, which shuttles glucose into the cells. Remember that in a stressful situation, one of the roles of cortisol is to increase the amount of fuel to the body. One of the ways it does this is by is by inhibiting or suppressing insulin so there is more free-floating glucose available to use. By suppressing insulin, cortisol, in effect, increases the amount of blood sugar available to the body.

Insulin resistance is a phrase used to describe abnormally low insulin sensitivity. Over time, cortisol increases the insulin resistance at the cellular level. The body responds by stimulating the pancreas to increase its production of insulin to rid the body of the excess glucose floating around in the bloodstream. High levels of insulin circulating in the blood are associated with heart failure, heart disease, obesity, high blood pressure, damage to blood vessels, and the development of type 2 diabetes. It makes you wonder if diabetes is running rampant due to poor diets or if diabetes is running rampant due to chronic levels of stress.

Cortisol also interferes with testosterone production because, in times of stress, all systems that have little to do with imminent survival are shut down. One of those systems (mentioned previously) is the reproductive system. Cortisol has been shown to decrease testosterone levels dramatically.[12] Cortisol even seems to block testosterone's well-known effect on competitiveness and dominance. In a study done at the University of Texas in 2010, the domains of leadership and competition were evaluated. Testosterone was positively related to dominance but only in those participants who had low cortisol levels. When it came to competition, the study participants were paired off in a game against each other. 100% of the participants who lost and wanted a rematch also had high testosterone and low cortisol levels. Interestingly, 100% of those with both high testosterone and high cortisol did not want a rematch.

In effect, high cortisol levels seem to block or reverse the testosterone—dominance relationship. The authors summed it up by stating, "The present studies provide the first empirical support for the claim that the neuroendocrine reproductive (HPG) and stress (HPA) axes interact to regulate dominance. Because dominance is related to gaining and maintaining high-status positions in social hierarchies, the finding suggests that only when cortisol is low should higher testosterone encourage higher status. When cortisol is high, higher testosterone may actually decrease dominance and in turn motivate lower status."[13]

When it comes to stress reduction and athletics, and I think it is fair to include life in general, the effects of chronically elevated cortisol cannot be underestimated. We should take every step necessary for the health of our clients, athletes, or patients to ensure a program that incorporates stress reduction as a part of the training process. By not doing so, we may very well be like driving a car down the road with one foot on the gas and one foot on the brake. The car may eventually get you to where you want to go, but it won't get you there efficiently and probably not safely.

Speaking of stress reduction in terms of managing adrenaline and cortisol, it should be noted that sleep deprivation, caffeine consumption, and alcohol consumption have each been shown to increase adrenaline and cortisol levels.

Mitigating the Human Stress Response

What are some ways we can mitigate the human stress response and possibly increase an athlete's performance? As a coach, you can encourage good lifestyle habits when your athletes are out of your presence. And, when they are with you, you can monitor their training intensities, their countenance, and their movements. Let's take a look at some effective ways to reduce the stress response and encourage recovery:

Diet and Exercise

- Take regular, planned breaks from prolonged intense training.
- Cycle the intensity, volume, and methods used.
- Use short bursts of exercise: 20 minutes of interval-type training works best to maximize training effects and lessen the effects of cortisol release.
- Avoid prolonged, intensive endurance training unless your sport of choice makes this form of exercise necessary.
- Consume carbohydrates and protein after exercise sessions
    - A ratio of 2:1 to 1:1 carbs to protein is suggested for strength training athletes.
    - Protein or branch-chain amino acids are preferred after a strength workout as they promote muscle growth and repair
- Eat a clean diet. Foods that are processed vs. organic tend to be nutrient-barren with a low bio-availability to the body.
- Decrease or eliminate alcohol and caffeine consumption

Rest

- Get 7 to 9 hours of sleep per night to decrease stress and cortisol release
    - A majority of HGH is released during the night when you sleep. The largest dose coming after the first period of stage 3 sleep, which is about an hour after you first fall asleep.

Socialization

- Don't isolate yourself; spend time with friends and family
  - Cortisol levels can be up to 50% higher in people who are isolated vs. those with a strong social network
  - Oxytocin is released when we feel connected to others
    - Known as the "love hormone" as it is released when we encounter physical closeness, touch, think of or even smell someone we for whom we feel love.
    - Being touched on the face, neck, shoulders, or back has been shown to elicit the production of oxytocin.
  - Stimulates the parasympathetic nervous system thus:
    - Improving digestion, immune system function
    - Decrease in heart rate, blood pressure, cortisol production

Spend Time Outside

- Industrial environments full of stimuli amp us up and put us on edge.
- Spending time outdoors helps us to decrease cortisol levels, lower blood pressure, and increases oxygenation and serotonin levels in the brain.

Regularly Participate in a Stress-Relieving Activity (Press RESET)

This is where Original Strength and engaging in The Three Pillars of Human Movement can have an extremely positive effect on the autonomic nervous system.

Diaphragmatic breathing - During the breath cycle, the sympathetic nervous system is stimulated on the inhale and the parasympathetic nervous system is stimulated on the exhale. The heart rate increases on each breath in and slows on each breath out. A long, slow exhale through the nose gives more time to utilize this simple facet of physiology to the benefit of the athlete. Along with the benefits we mentioned at the beginning of the book, breathing properly with the diaphragm relieves excess muscle tension and muscle guarding; it relaxes the body. Taking deliberate, focused breaths also melts away tension, stress, anger, and fear. It helps to calm the emotions, so they don't kidnap the thoughts and derail both mental and physical performance, or worse. Breathing is the best place to go when the sympathetic nervous system is overwhelmed.

Activating the Vestibular System - Head movements, rolling, and rocking are also very therapeutic and soothing to the mind. For example, rocking, like smiling, triggers the brain to release endorphins, the feel-good hormones. These hormones have the effect of relieving pain and inducing feelings of pleasure. Since the beginning of time, mothers have used rocking and swaying to soothe their children's emotions. Rocking still works to soothe children of all ages and sizes.

Similarly, rolling also soothes the mind and elicits a great effect on the overall health of the body by promoting healthy pituitary function. In fact, tactile stimulation has been shown to be a crucial factor in healthy pituitary function.[14] The pituitary is responsible for growth hormone production, which is essential for the growth and development of muscle and connective tissue. The pituitary gland is also involved with and affected by the release of adrenaline and cortisol due to the hypothalamic pituitary adrenal (HPA) axis, the system responsible for releasing adrenaline and cortisol in response to stress. Rolling may help reduce and mitigate the stress being perceived by the brain, promoting a healthy pituitary gland through the reduction of adrenaline and cortisol and through the stimulation of the skin.

Crawling - Crawling, as instructed in Original Strength, can be done at slow, medium, or fast speeds; all of them are great. But when we want to affect our body's hormone levels, in this case, cortisol, slow methodical movement wins the day. Slow movement requiring grace and fine motor skill is associated with an area of the brain that also secretes a hormone called GABA (gamma-aminobutyric acid). GABA is a neurotransmitter in the brain that helps block unwanted stimuli and helps us to maintain focus and concentration. Many of the clients that I work with find that baby crawling is a very therapeutic, cathartic experience.

By regularly engaging the Big 5 RESETs and training in a way that honors The Three Pillars of Human Movement (diaphragmatic breathing, vestibular system stimulation, and midline crossing or contralateral movements), you reduce stress, taking the breaks off of movement and optimizing posture. Again, everything about a person is intertwined. The better a person moves, the better a person feels, and the better a person's thoughts and mental abilities. Moving well, Pressing RESET, is a powerful way to reduce stress.

The Human Stress Response Can Also Be Good

What? Can stress also be a good thing? Well, yes. Everything in life has a purpose. Stress in the proper dosage can be very beneficial to athletic performance. Check out this passage from Thomas Kurtz:

"The sympathetic system, which mobilizes catabolic reactions for energy production, should dominate during effort and the parasympathetic system which mobilizes anabolic reactions for rebuilding the energy stores and body structures, should dominate during rest. A sympathetic system that is overly active at rest keeps an athlete from restoring his or her work capacity; a parasympathetic system dominating at work makes it impossible for the athlete to mobilize her or himself for intensive efforts (Isreal 1976). . . . An optimal state of athletic form exists when the sympathetic system clearly dominates at work, and the parasympathetic at rest. The greater the spread between them, and the more rapid the change of the dominating system from work to rest, the better."[15]

The last part of that quote is the heavy hitter: ". . . an optimal state of athletic form exists . . ." It's this optimal state of athletic form or arousal that athletes are constantly striving for in competition, and it's the nervous system that governs this state of being. When everything comes together, when the level of stress is just enough but not too much, we tend to see optimal performance.

The ultimate purpose of the stress response is to get us ready to move. We know that the amount of adrenaline and cortisol released is dose dependent on the level of stress imposed on the organism. Then, through practice, it is possible to control the amount of excitation or good stress that can aid in physical performance. When the level of excitation is optimal for the task at hand, this is called the Optimal State of Arousal.

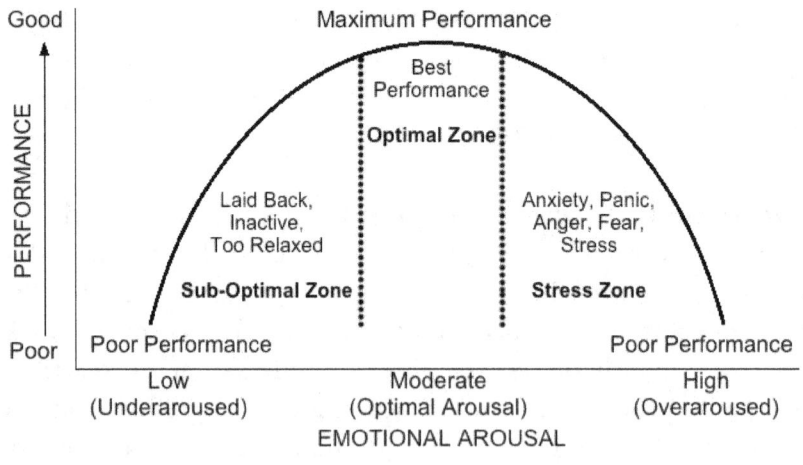

Figure 6

The above graph is an illustration of the Yerkes-Dodson law, which shows the relationship between arousal and performance. Initially developed in 1908 by psychologists Robert M. Yerkes and John Dillingham Dodson, the law states that performance for a given task gets better as the individual becomes more aroused—but only to a certain point. After that point, the performance gets worse with more stress.[16]

Obviously, there can be many types of tasks applied to this model. Cognitive/intellectual tasks, where concentration is necessary, seem to improve with lower levels of arousal, whereas physical tasks that require endurance of effort seem to improve more with higher levels of arousal. In other words, the shape of the curve can vary depending on the task at hand. The takeaway here for coaches is that everything we impose on the athletes we work with has a stress level to it and that stress level can be theoretically optimized for peak performance.

Looking at Figure 6, the Optimal Arousal Zone is obviously where we want our athletes to be. This is the area where the perfect amount of stress gets them engaged, enthused, and motivated. In this zone, the right amount of the stress hormones adrenaline and cortisol, along with beneficial brain chemicals like dopamine, are mobilized and aid in the athlete's ability to get the job done effectively and optimally. Again, adrenaline and cortisol only become harmful when their dose is too great due to the perceived stress or when they are chronically released due to an overly dominating sympathetic nervous system. Good stress, or the appropriate response to stress, can be good when it comes to optimal performance, survival, and the overall enjoyment of life.

Manipulating the Stress Response Using Original Strength

Incorporating Original Strength, The Three Pillars of Human Movement, and Pressing RESET can play a major role in getting athletes prepared for competition as well as helping them come back to a parasympathetic state after a hard session, event, or game. This is especially important for athletes who participate in multiple events on the same day.

Before we talk about recovery, let's talk about preparing to perform. When getting an athlete ready for training, practice, or competition, the warm-up or prep is invaluable as it prepares the nervous system and the brain for what is to come. I believe a good warm-up should consist of the following four phases:

1. Original Strength Resets
   - These can include progressions and regressions based on the athlete's individual needs.

2. Non-specific warm-up to increase body temperature
   - Approximately five minutes of continuous or semi-continuous movement(s), or until the sweat response is noted.
     - This is a great place to work on Original Strength movement flows (flowing and moving from one reset to another).

3. Active-dynamic movements
   - These are various movements that take the athlete's body through multiple planes of motion and varied dimensions at varied speeds.

4. Specific movements that relate to the main body of the training session, practice session, competition, or game.

From an Original Strength Performance-enhancing mindset, the purpose of the warm-up is to prime the nervous system for action by:

- Stimulating the reflexive stability of the core via diaphragmatic breathing
- Linking together the X of the body via contralateral or midline crossing movements
- Stimulating the vestibular system
- Increasing the elasticity and contractibility of muscles

- Creating greater efficiency of the respiratory and cardiovascular systems
- Shortening reaction time
- Improving proprioception
- Improving concentration
- Improving coordination
- Regulating emotional states (especially before competition)

Beyond serving as a warm-up, or movement prep, Original Strength can also be used to help athletes who are in the sub-optimal zone of the Yerkes-Dodson Curve (Figure 6). These are athletes who have a difficult time getting mentally and physically prepared for competition. This type of athlete needs simple and easy resets: fast movements conducted with enthusiasm to help increase the sympathetic drive. Some examples of this are:

- Quick cross-crawls or vigorous skin raking and cross body slapping and limb shaking
- Marching with a quick step, as if the floor were hot
- Skipping
- Spider-man or Leopard crawling

Getting the athlete ready for action and getting up into the Optimal Arousal Zone is only part of the performance puzzle. There is also the cool-down, come-down, and recovery piece to consider. This is an easy area to dismiss when it comes to performance enhancement. Do not make this mistake. The ability to recover greatly affects athletic performance. This is not only true between multiple competitions, but it's also true from training session to training session and from day to day.

For athletes who compete multiple times in a day or week, having the ability to come down from competition is just as important as the ability to ramp up for competition. It preserves valuable mental, emotional, and physical energy. In other words, it helps them recover so they can perform well again. Again, recovery is essential for optimal performance. Keeping the Yerkes-Dodson performance curve in mind (Figure 6), let's look at how using Original Strength can help an athlete get to, or return, to the Optimal Arousal/Performance Zone.

The overly excited or over-stressed athlete needs slow RESETs and movements that require precision and complexity to get them closer to the Optimal Arousal Zone for optimal performance. Slow movements may also help the athlete to calm down via the release of GABA. Remember, GABA helps us focus and stay calm. It has an inhibitory effect on the nervous system and helps us to block out non-essential stimuli. It is released during engaging activity and at night to block out stimuli that would keep us awake. The areas of the brain that are associated with GABA release are associated closely with movement, in particular fine, coordinated movements.

Again, the goal is to bring the over-stressed athlete back down, dampening the sympathetic drive (stress), and helping them to get back into a more parasympathetic, anabolic (or maybe less catabolic) state. Slow and steady wins the race back from an overly sympathetic nervous system.

Here are some examples that could be useful in returning the athlete to the Optimal Arousal Zone:

- Slow and focused diaphragmatic breathing
- Slow baby crawls and bird dogs
- Rocking (with all its variations),
- Rolling regressions such as half rolls, egg rolls, rocking chairs, wipers

The above examples can also be quite useful for a general cool-down that can lead to a quicker recovery, allowing for a better performance in the days to come.

When it comes to manipulating the stress response to help your athletes achieve their best performance, another variable to consider is you. Knowing where your athlete's mind is, where their emotions are, what state their nervous system is in, knowing what their body needs, and knowing how to help them get to the place they need to be to perform is mostly dependent on you. In fact, you could possess the greatest and most influential variable when it comes to helping your athletes achieve optimal performance.

THE GREATEST PERFORMANCE VARIABLE

". . . And what does the Lord require of you but to do justly, to love mercy, and to walk humbly with your God?"

—Micah 6:8

As mentioned earlier, as a coach, you possess the one thing that can mitigate many of the internal stressors the athlete has. You may very well be the ultimate external performance enhancer for your athletes. You can influence their autonomic nervous system, their thoughts, and their emotions, through your most powerful coaching tool—love.

Love is power. In fact, it is the greatest superpower known to man. We are talking about real love here: unconditional, gentle, kind, patient, humble, and genuine care for another. This type of love knows no bounds and no obstacles. It removes barriers and limits. When your athlete knows you care about them, you not only remove the barriers between you and your athlete, you remove the limits in their mind—the doubt, the anger, the frustration, the fears, and the anxiety. Notice those are all toxic states of the mind and the emotions. They all pour into the sympathetic nervous system, and they are all exasperated by it as well. They are devastating to health, performance, and sanity. Your willingness to love your athlete, to care about them, to see them, can help remove those toxic states from their mind and produce an athlete without limits; one who will not only perform at a higher level but one who will perform for you because you care for them. Genuine love is a performance enhancer, and it flows both ways.

This may sound absurd, but if you want to optimize your athletes' or your team's performance, you must invest in them through love. If you only see stats, reps, sets, figures, percentages, cycles, schedules, and salaries, you will never truly optimize your athletes' ability to perform. Just as The Three Pillars of Human Movement are the reflexive foundation for all movement expression and performance, love, or lack of love, is the reflexive foundation of your ability to LEAD your athletes. Your influence, how you LEAD, will greatly affect the level at which your athletes will rise and perform on the field of play, and perhaps more importantly, on the field of life.

If this is a new thought to you, let us help you learn how to LEAD.

The Three Keys to LEAD

1) Do Justly or Do Your Best

If you want to LEAD and help your athletes become their best, you must first do your best. To do your best is to put them first. After all, it's not about you. You have to put their best interest first. To do this, you may have to ask yourself some questions like:

"What does my athlete need right now?" Or "What do I really want for my athlete?"

You may even have to ask hard questions like, "Can I do what is best for my athlete and still do what is best for my team?"

Sometimes, asking questions like this can help bring clarity and offer the best course of action to take regarding how you can best love your athlete.

Doing your best and taking your best course of action toward your athletes can lead you down many paths. It may lead you to learn all you can or learn something new and open yourself up to new ideas such as Original Strength, learning new techniques and methodologies that can develop them physically, safely, and effectively. Or, it may simply lead you to listen to your athlete talk about a challenge he or she is facing at home.

Whatever your course of action, whatever you do—do your best. In other words, love them. Simple enough, right? Maybe. But to really love your athletes, you have to be able to "see" them.

2) Love, Mercy, or "See" Your Athletes

Athletes are people. They are someone's son or daughter. They often don't have a great deal of confidence in themselves. When a LEADer, a mentor, a friend, sees them and believes in them, it can greatly influence and bolster their confidence. Often, knowing a coach values them and believes in them inspires them to perform at a level greater than they would otherwise be capable of. When an athlete plays for a coach or a team member, they are playing for something greater than themselves. In other words, if an athlete knows you see them, they begin to be able to see you, too. They'll perform for you as well as themselves.

This idea goes far beyond improving the performance of an athlete on the field or in the weight room. If you learn to see other people and do your best for them, you will greatly affect how they perform in life and improve their chance of success in all areas of life. You will also influence them to see others and do their best toward others. This is movement that changes the world.

Again, to put your athletes best interest first, you must be able to see them. This may be easier said than done because many of us are smoke and mirrors; we role play through all of our interactions with other people. We display and perform for the expectations of those we encounter, and we are judged accordingly. But few of us are ever really seen through non-judging, accepting eyes for who we really are. As a result, most all of our interactions are shallow and even fake. The roles we play with one another, and the judgments we make with one another, create barriers that prevent us from having any true relationships with others. In other words, we don't see real people; we see the roles they play.

You may be wondering, if others are playing a role, and not being genuine, how can we truly see them? We can't unless we are willing to lay down our judgments, the lens from which we see them. If we really want to see our athletes, we have to be able to look through their performance. We have to learn to look at them through a lens of love. By the way, the lens we often view others through, the one that gives us the eyes of judgment is called the ego.

3) Walk Humbly or Be Humble

Be humble. We've all heard this. We all know being humble is the way to be. Yet, many of us don't actually walk in humility—not fully, anyway. This may be because most of us don't even know what humility is, and it also may be because walking in humility isn't necessarily easy.

First off, what is humility? Humility is defined as a modest or low view of one's own importance. The problem with this very common definition is that it often leads people into false humility. We know we should be modest or humble, so we purposefully try to lower ourselves and not take credit for things we actually may be responsible for. This is only one example of false humility. There are others, but I'm trying to illustrate how the common working definition of humility is often misused. It results in non-genuine actions. What if a better definition of humility was simply being who you are (being genuine) in all of your interactions with others? What if humility was synonymous with integrity—no falsehoods, no roles, just the real you.

And here is where humility gets hard. We have an internal humility saboteur. This saboteur not only fights to prevent us from being genuine, it also strives to give us a lens of judgment, a lens tinted by fear. You may have heard of this saboteur before. It is often referred to as ego.

The reason we role play, the reason we judge others, the reason we lie, the reason we withhold the truth, and the reason for most of our shortcomings is our ego. Fueled by fear or lack, our ego strives to protect itself by maintaining its importance through many means. It strives to be right and prove others wrong, it draws hard lines in the sand of either/or, and it refuses to see the middle or the other side in any circumstance. It rages when others disrespect us with a gesture, a comment, or a lane change, and it makes up stories and motives of all of the other people we interact with. In short, our ego disallows us to truly see others for who they really are because it is focused on itself, and it is afraid of diminishing. As a result, our ego also disallows us to be who we truly are. It is the enemy within, and it is a clever saboteur.

Have you ever done anything you didn't want to do or something you knew you shouldn't have done as soon as you did it? Have you ever flipped someone off in traffic and felt bad about it a second later? Have you ever watched your athlete's lips moving, but you couldn't hear what they were saying because you were playing a different narrative in your head about what they really did, or about how they were lazy and didn't listen to you? That's ego; that's not you.

The ego is why it is so hard to be your true self and walk in humility. We all want to be genuine, and we all want to see others and love others. And we can do these things when we are awake and aware. It takes being awake, being alert to who we are, to lay our ego aside. When we can lay our ego aside, we can then walk in humility.

Humility allows you to see beyond yourself. It allows you to *be* beyond yourself. It allows you to truly live life because you're not holding on to your own life. When we allow our ego to rise, we limit our own potential and that of everyone else around us. But if we are alert, if we hold fast to who we are, we can catch these egoic moments and let them go. This is key to true LEADership.

LEAD

If we want to improve our athletes' performance, if we want to impact the world around us, we must learn how to decrease ourselves and increase others. We must learn how to Lay Ego Aside Daily. This is what it means to be humble or genuine. This is what it means to LEAD, and this is how we make a difference in the lives of our athletes.

Lay
Ego
Aside
Daily

This is a layered performance enhancer. It will help enhance the performance of your athletes, but it will enhance your own performance as well. When you LEAD, you will become more effective as a coach, a husband, a wife, a dad, a mom, or a friend. When you LEAD, you create life-changing movement, a different kind of movement that makes the entire world better.

LEAD. This is how you love others. This is how you do your best, how you open your eyes to be able to see others, and how you are able to walk in humility. This is how you change the world through movement. This is also how you express your genuine self and optimize your performance.

You were created to LEAD, to lay your ego aside daily, to decrease yourself and lift up each other.

This is love. In fact, there is no greater love. There is no greater performance enhancer either. LEAD on.

IN THE END...

"What is truth?"

—Pontius Pilate

The truth is, there are potentially endless factors and variables that affect athletic performance. We are humans, awesomely made and wonderfully complex. We have minds, emotions, thoughts, environments, circumstances, situations, outlooks, backgrounds, histories, climates, cultures, social influences, genetics, physical structures, opportunities, shortfalls, beliefs, support, wills, personalities, nutrition habits, and bodies. All of these and so much more affect our ability to perform on any given day, in any given moment, to the best or the least of our abilities.

The goal of this book is to give you a foundation, a concrete place to stand when trying to improve your performance or the performance of those you train. For all of the variables that you cannot control, there are quite a few you can influence through honoring the movement design of the body. The rest can be influenced by honoring the individual.

We believe the best and most effective route to increase athletic performance is through:

1) Pressing RESET by engaging in The Three Pillars of Human Movement. This can be done by remembering and revisiting the five main movements of the developmental sequence: breathing, head control, rolling, rocking, and crawling.

2) Learning how to manage and maintain diaphragmatic breathing during moments of intense physical stress.

3) Adding load, or resistance, to the natural gait pattern in any of its forms.

4) Performing awkward carries of all types.

5) Strength training by contra-laterally loading the X, also known as tying the X together.

6) Recognizing when the athlete's nervous system is sympathetically dominant or parasympathetically driven.

7) Knowing when and how to upregulate the athlete's nervous system and when to downregulate the athlete's nervous system.

8) Ensuring the athlete is recovering through Pressing RESET, getting nutritious meals, getting restorative sleep, and managing mental, emotional, and physical stress levels.

9) LEADing

Looking at this list, it can probably be summarized further by stating that you are the greatest performance enhancement variable. When it comes to improving how you move, and how your athletes move, honor your heart and honor your design. The performance will be there. It is already inside each of us, waiting to be expressed.

BIBLIOGRAPHY

1. https://www.ncbi.nlm.nih.gov/pmc/articles/PMC3940506/

2. https://www.atsjournals.org/doi/full/10.1164/rccm.2205014

3. https://www.sciencedirect.com/science/article/pii/S0014488614003537

4. https://www.sciencedirect.com/science/article/pii/S0014488614003537

5. Movement Matters, Katy Bowman; Propriometric Press, 2016

6. Intervention: Course Corrections for the Athlete and Trainer, Dan John; On target Publications, 2011

7. Movement Restoration, Brandon Hetzler

8. Pressing RESET:Original Strength Reloaded, Tim Anderson and Geoff Neupert, FontLife Publications, 2015

9. https://www.ncbi.nlm.nih.gov/pubmed/25028798

10. https://www.merriam-webster.com/dictionary/stability

11. Carla Hannaford, Smart Moves (Salt Lake City: Great River Books, 2005) p. 176.

12. Acute Suppression of Circulating Testosterone Levels by Cortisol in Men, D.C. Cumming, M.E. Quigley, S.S.C. Yen, Journal of Clinical Endocrinology and Metabolism Vol 57, Issue 3, 1 Sept 1983 pp 671-673.

13. Testosterone and cortisol jointly regulate dominance: Evidence for a dual – hormone hypothesis, Mehta, Pranjal and Josephs, Robert. Hormones and Behavior Volume 58, Issue 5 Nov 2010 pp 898 – 906.

14. Juhan, Job's Body, a Handbook for Bodywork (Barrytown: Barrytown/Station Hill Press, 2003), p. 85.

15. Kurtz, Science of Sports Training. How to Plan and Control Training for Peak Performance (Island Pond, Vermont: Stadion Publishing Company, 2001), p. 15.

16. https://en.wikipedia.org/wiki/Yerkes–Dodson_law

ABOUT THE AUTHORS

Tim Anderson is co-creator of the Original Strength System, a physical restoration system. Tim has also authored several books including Pressing Reset: Original Strength Reloaded, Habitual Strength, and Original Strength Restoration. He travels all around the world teaching the Original Strength System to health, fitness and educational professionals. Tim has held various ACE certifications since 1998, NASM Performance Enhancement Specialist since 2014, Battling Ropes Certified Coach 1 and 2, CK-FMS and FMS-2009, Z-Health R, I, S, T-2008, RKC 1 and 2-2006, SFG -2012.

Chip Morton serves as the Bengals Head Strength and Conditioning Coach, a position he has held since 2003. During his tenure, Chip and his staff have established a program that continues to include innovative ideas while keeping its roots grounded in fundamental principles of productive training. Chip is in his 27th NFL season, including serving as Assistant Strength and Conditioning Coach with the San Diego Chargers (1992-94) and Baltimore Ravens (1999-2001) and Head Strength and Conditioning Coach with the Carolina Panthers (1995-98) and Washington Redskins (2002). He has coached with two Super Bowl teams—the 1994 Chargers and the 2000 Ravens. Prior to the NFL, Chip was an Assistant Strength Coach at Ohio State (1985-86) while completing his Master's Degree in Physical Education. In 1987, he became the first-ever full-time Strength and Conditioning Assistant for Nittany Lions football team. He also worked with 14 other men's and women's sports during his five years (1987-91) at Penn State. In 2016, Chip became an Original Strength Certified Coach; he is also certified in the Stick Mobility system of training. Chip is a Level One Sports Performance Coach through the United States Weightlifting Association and has been a Certified Strength & Conditioning Specialist (C.S.C.S.) in the National Strength & Conditioning Association since 1990. In 2006, Morton became the first NFL strength coach to receive the Russian Kettlebell Instructor's Certification (RKC), and in '08, he was certified as a Level I coach in John Brookfield's Battling Ropes training system.

Mark Shropshire is the President and CEO of Shropshire Sports Training located in Columbia, Maryland. He has been training athletes and other professionals for 23 years. Mark has had the opportunity to work with and consult a wide variety of athletes in his career which includes members of the NFL, MLB, NHL, Professional Soccer, US Marshals, US Secret Service, SWAT, Department of Defense Emergency Regional Response Team, Naval Special Warfare, Army Special Operations, as well as numerous individuals who play college sports at the Division I, II and III levels.

Previously Mark was the Director of Cal Ripken Jr. Sports Acceleration from 1998 – 2002. Mark has been active with Original Strength since 2012, writing blogs and instructing other professionals nationally since 2015. Mark earned a Masters in Human Performance from the University of Montana in 1998. He is a Level II FMS and CKFMS practitioner and a Black Belt in Tae Kwon Do.

Learn More About Original Strength

Original Strength is an education company focusing on helping health and fitness professionals optimize the results seen by their patients and clients. In addition to workshops for everyday athletes and business professionals, we offer certification workshops geared specifically towards health and fitness professions, such as Physical and Occupational Therapists, Orthopedic Professionals, Chiropractors, Body and Scar Tissue Professionals, Athletic Trainers, Personal Trainers and many other professions.

We invite you to visit our website at OriginalStrength.Net for more information. While on our site, please check out our MovementSnax videos. These are short videos of RESETs you can do anytime throughout your day.

We also offer a number of books and a DVD to take you from good to better to best.

OS Pressing RESET - Original Strength Reloaded
Original Strength Restoration
Original Strength for the Tactical Athlete
Habitual Strength

An Introduction to Pressing RESET - DVD

All are available at OriginalStrength.net/shop or Amazon.com

To find a workshop near you visit OriginalStrength.Net/events.

To find an Original Strength Certified Professional near you; visit https://originalstrength.net/find-a-certified-coach/

"...I am fearfully and wonderfully made..."
Psalm 139:14

www.ingramcontent.com/pod-product-compliance
Lightning Source LLC
Chambersburg PA
CBHW052059070526
44584CB00017B/2248